EROTIC ART PHOTOGRAPHY

VOL. 6

LESBOS

1890 – 1930

JANSSEN

P.O.BOX 404, SIMONS' TOWN, 7995, SOUTH AFRICA

PRODUCTION: DRUCK- UND VERLAGSHAUS ERFURT GMBH

PRINTED IN GERMANY

DISTRIBUTION: LKG, PÖTZSCHAUER WEG, D-04579 ESPENHAIN, GERMANY

DISTRIBUTION USA:
JANSSEN PUBLISHERS, 41, MONROE TURNPIKE, TRUMBULL, CONNECTICUT 06611

ISBN: 0-9584314-9 -3

EMAIL PUBLISHERS OFFICE: JANSSENP@IAFRICA.COM

PLEASE VISIT OUR WEBSITE UNDER: **WWW.JANSSENBOOKS.CO.ZA**

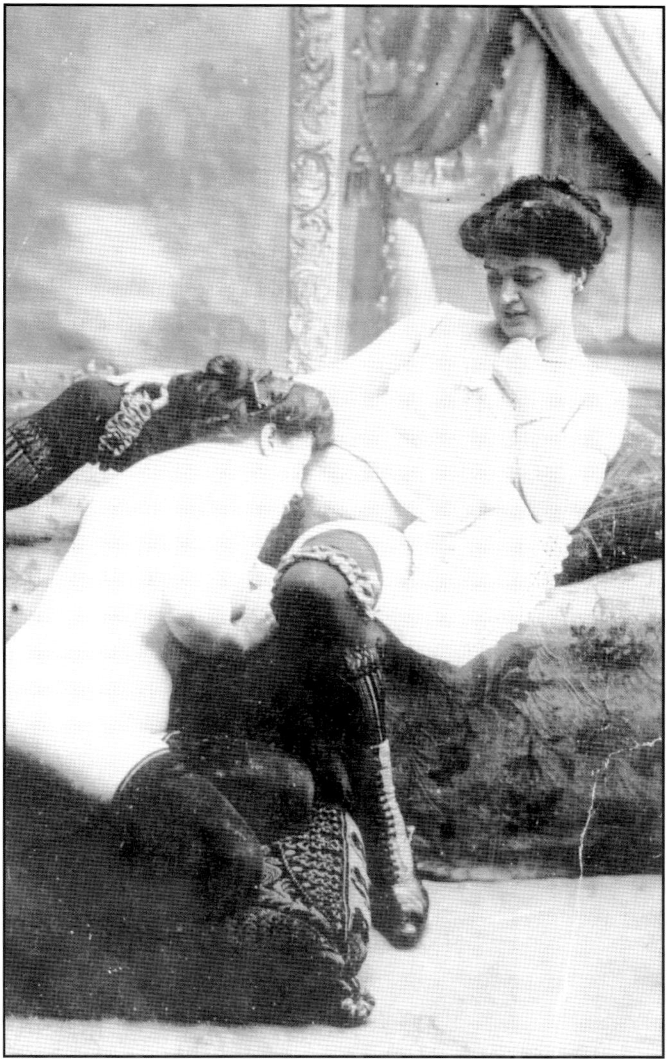

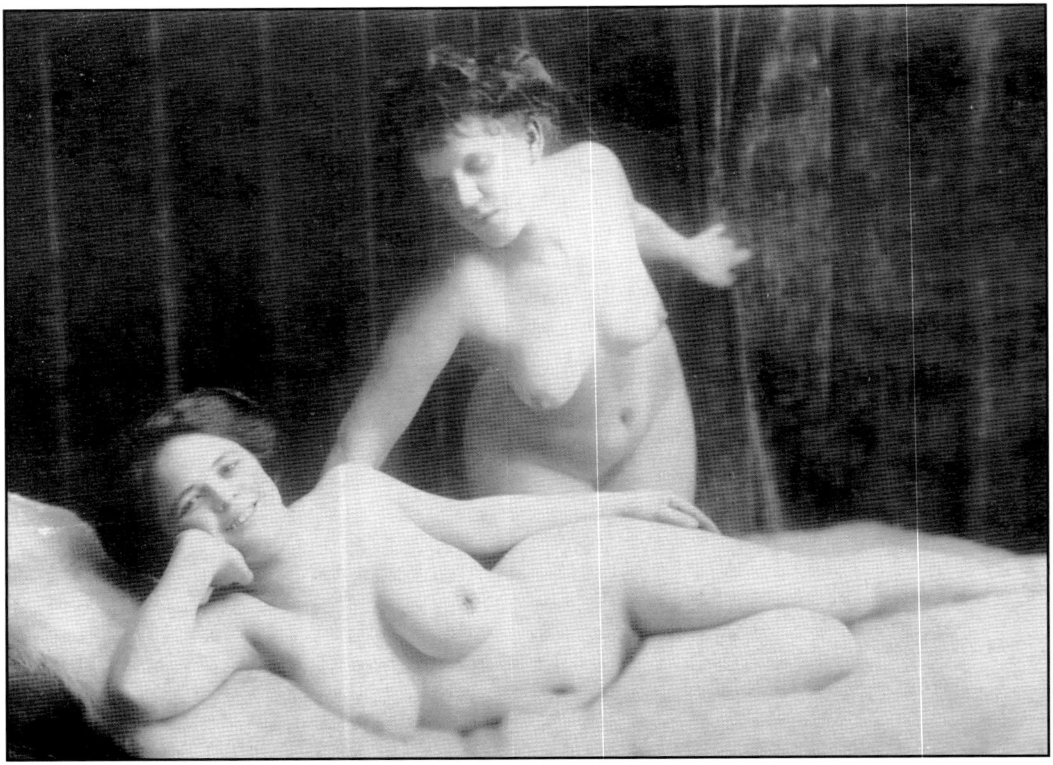

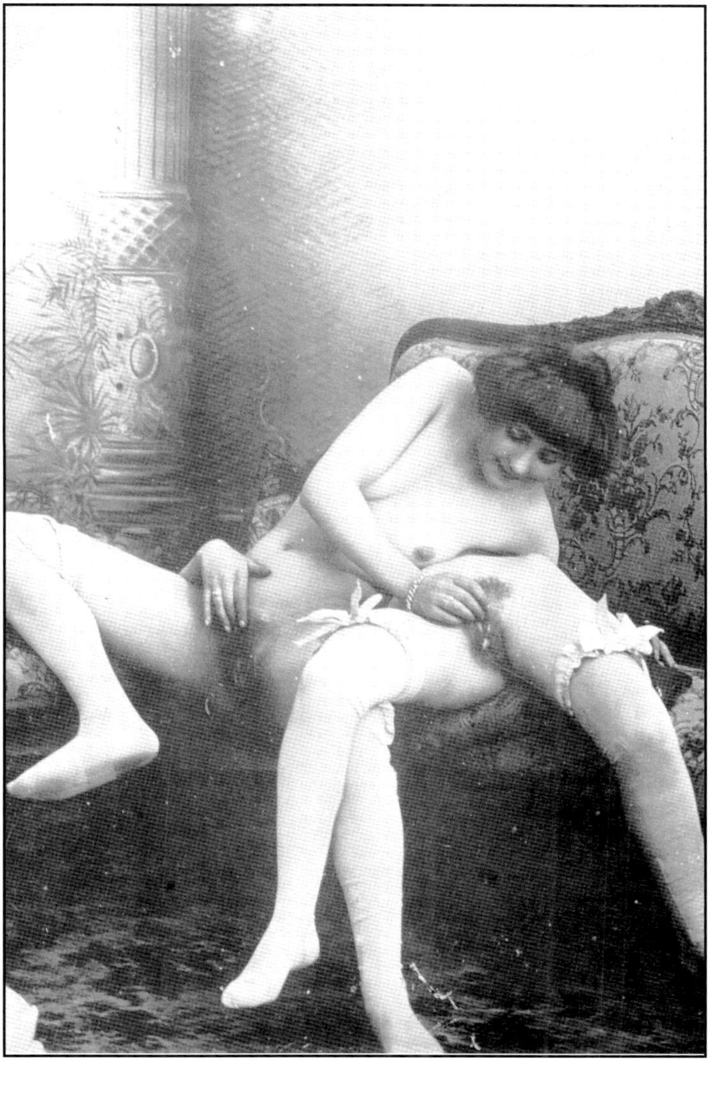

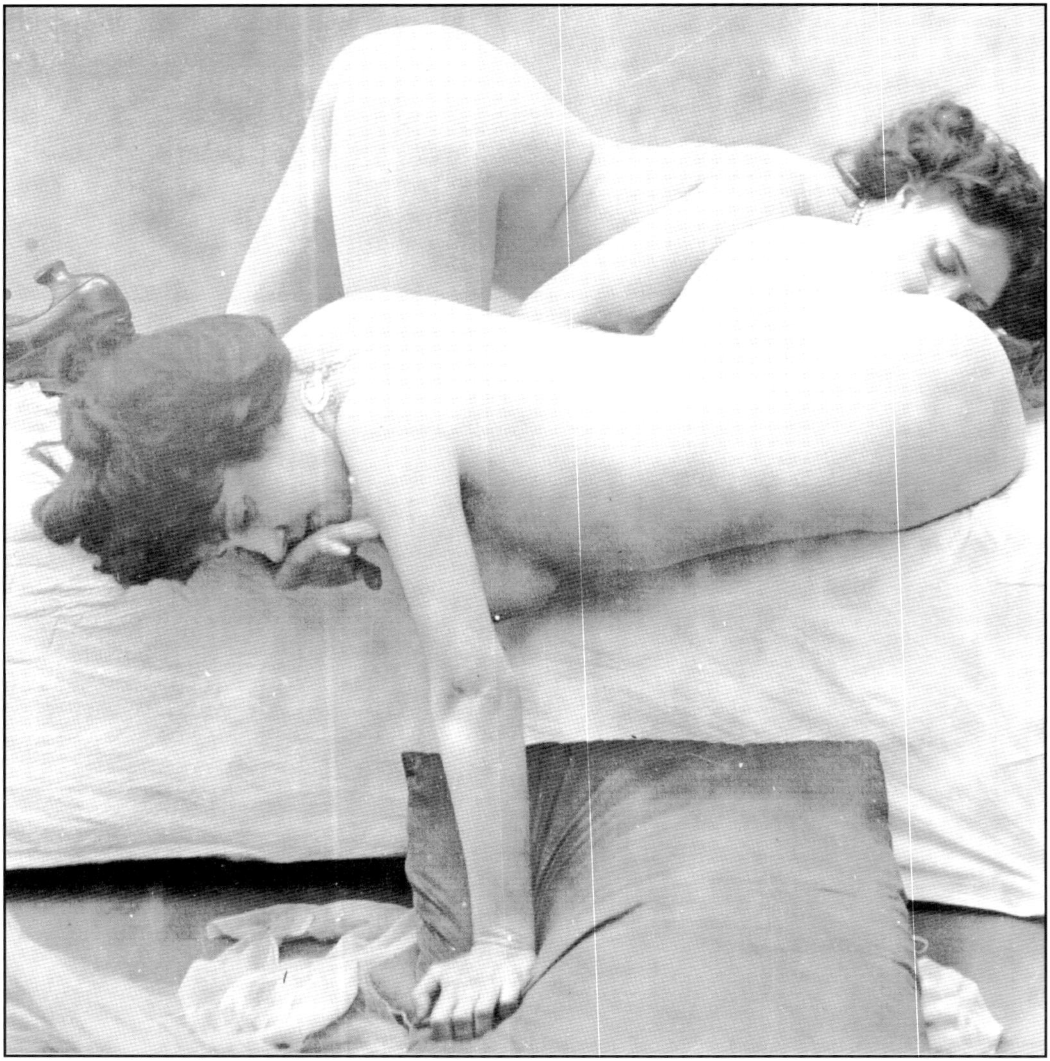

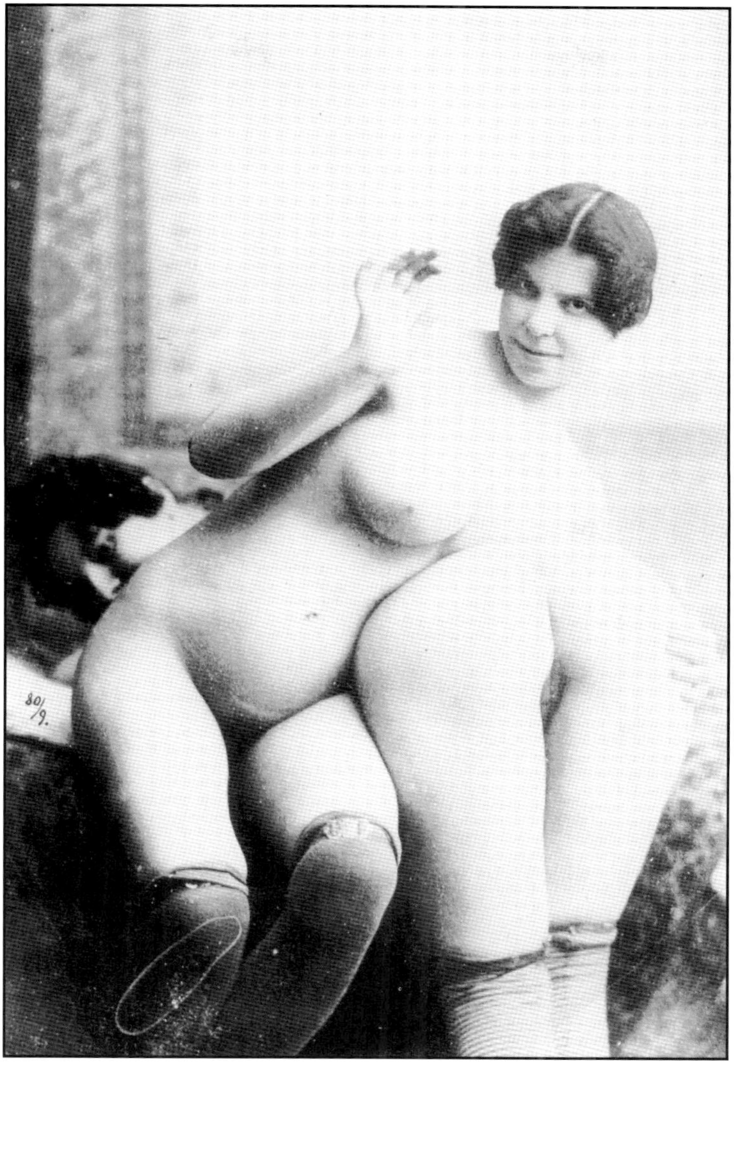
80/9.

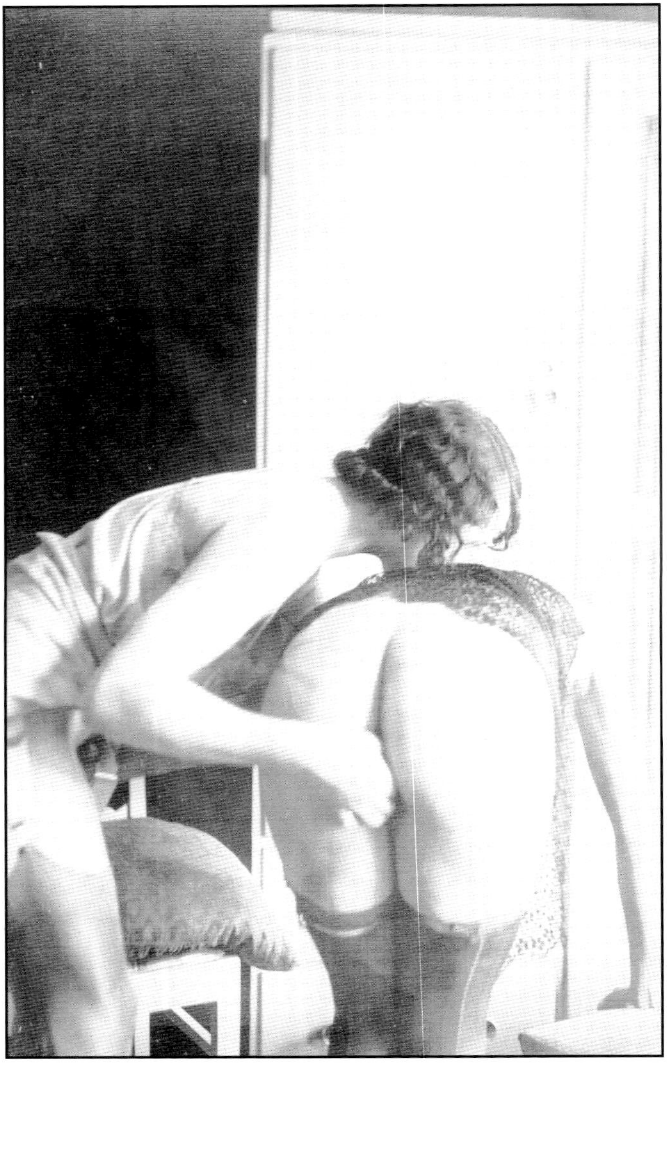

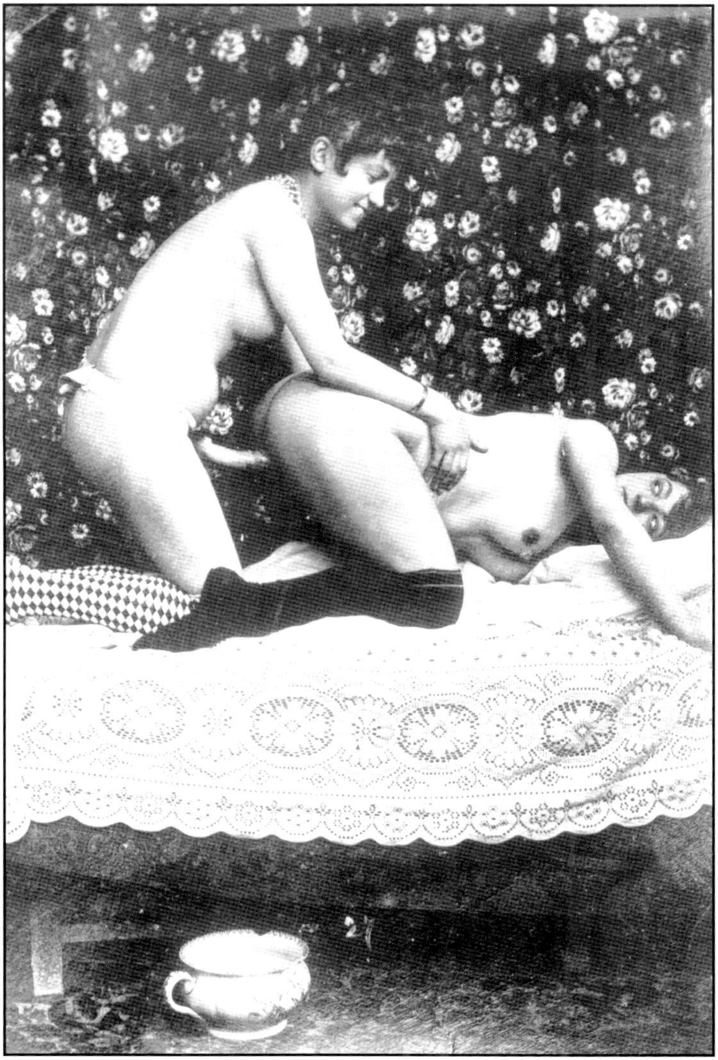

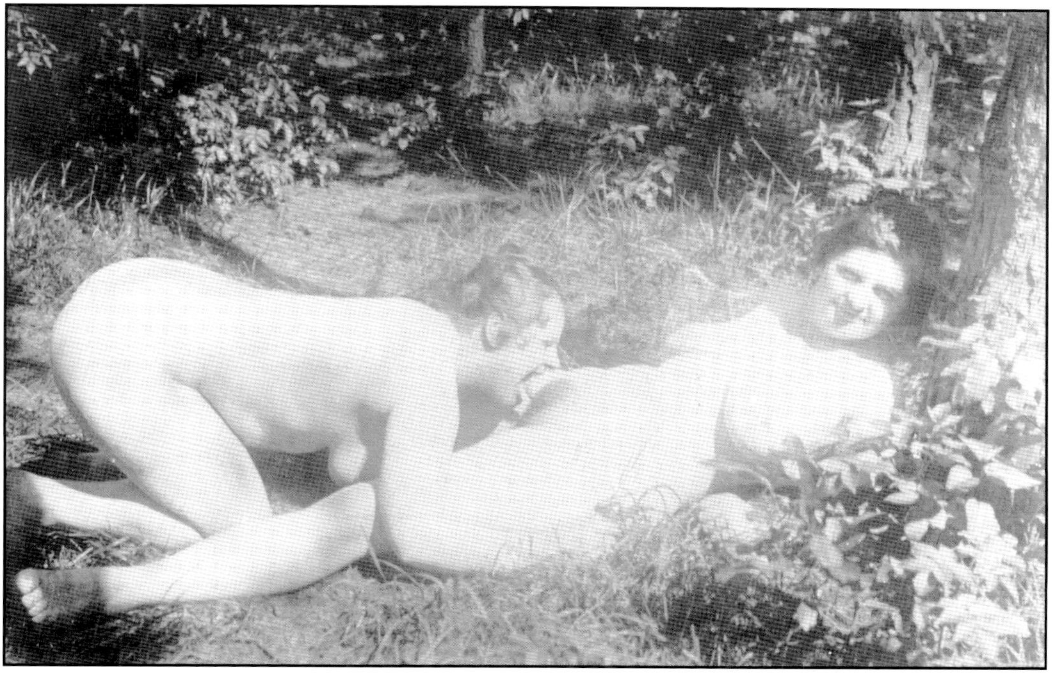

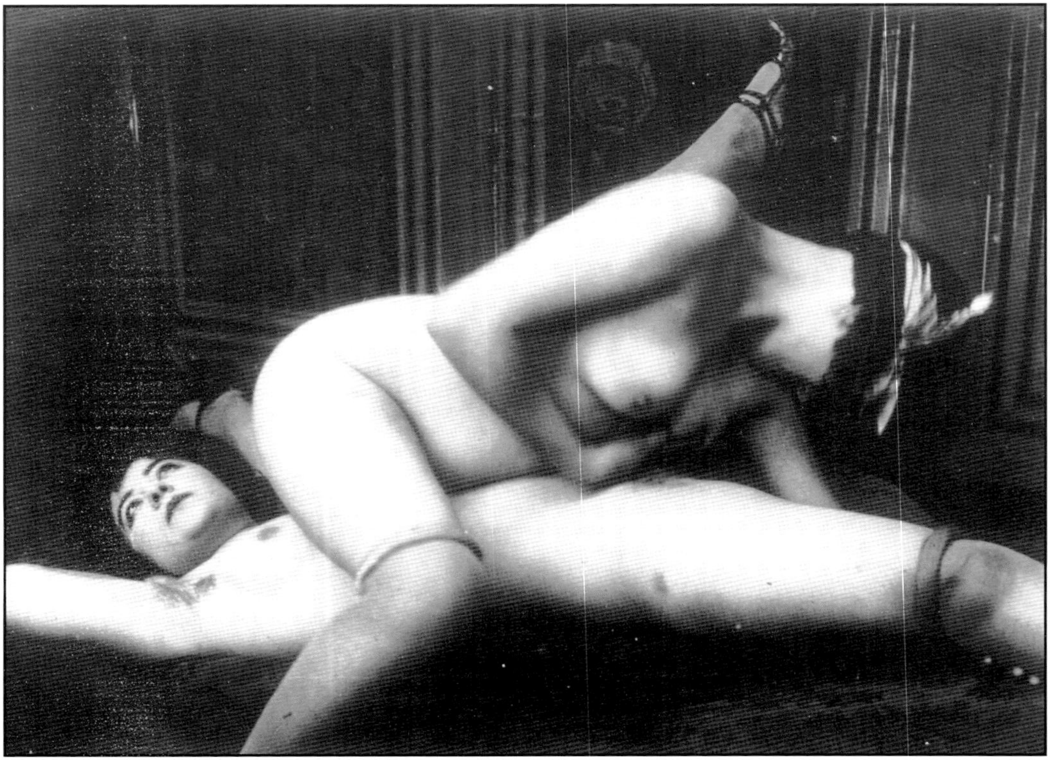

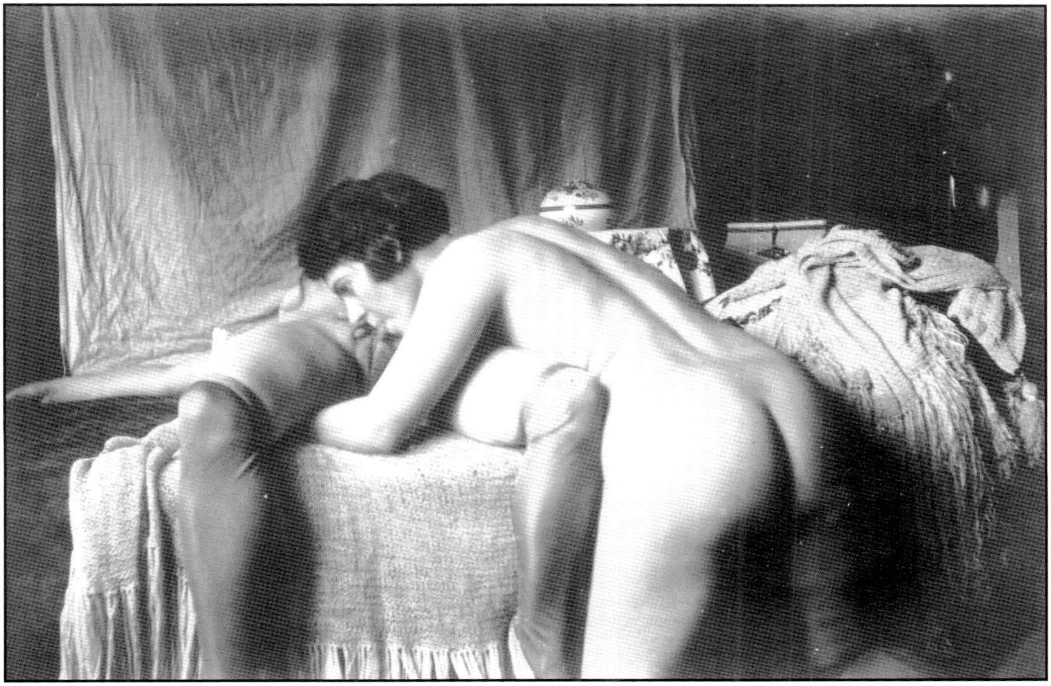

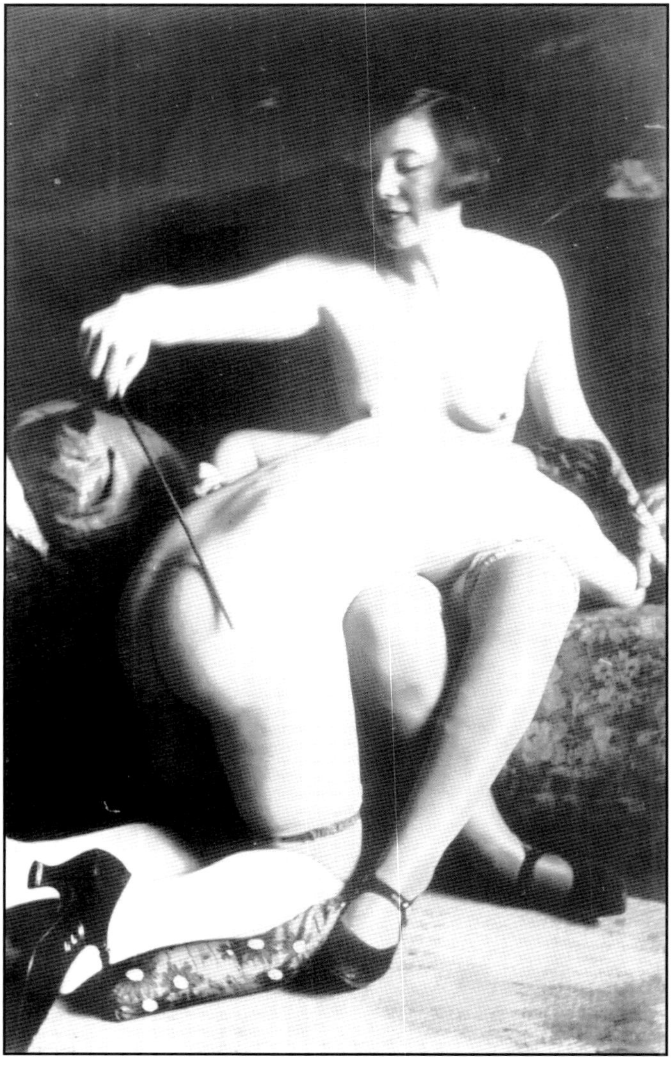

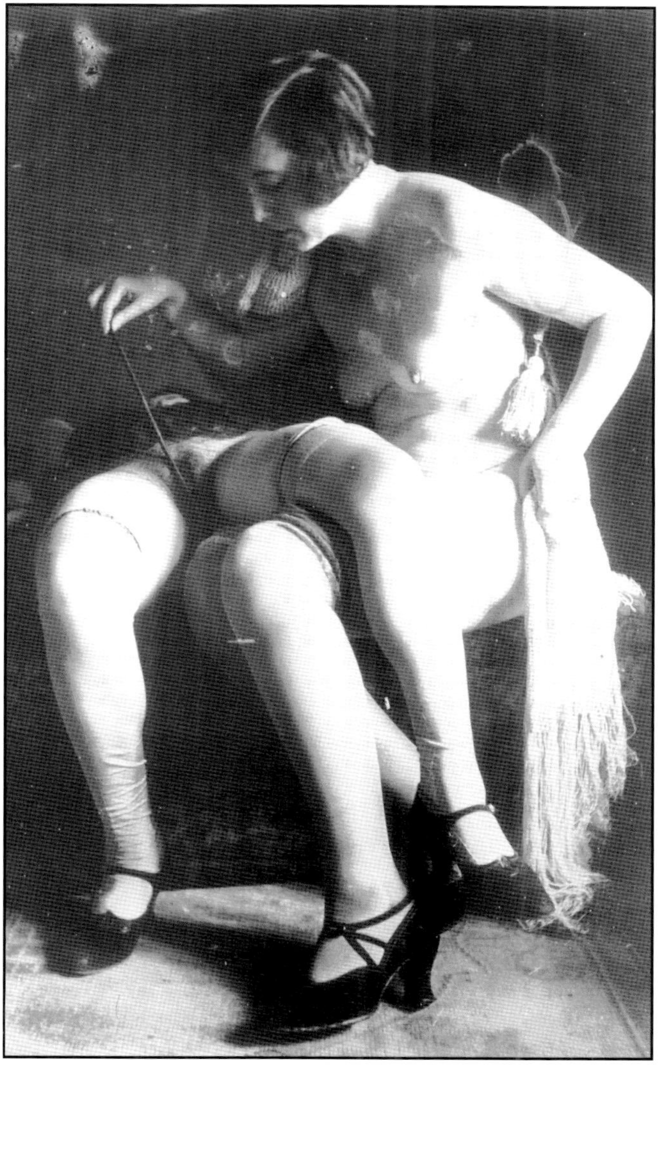

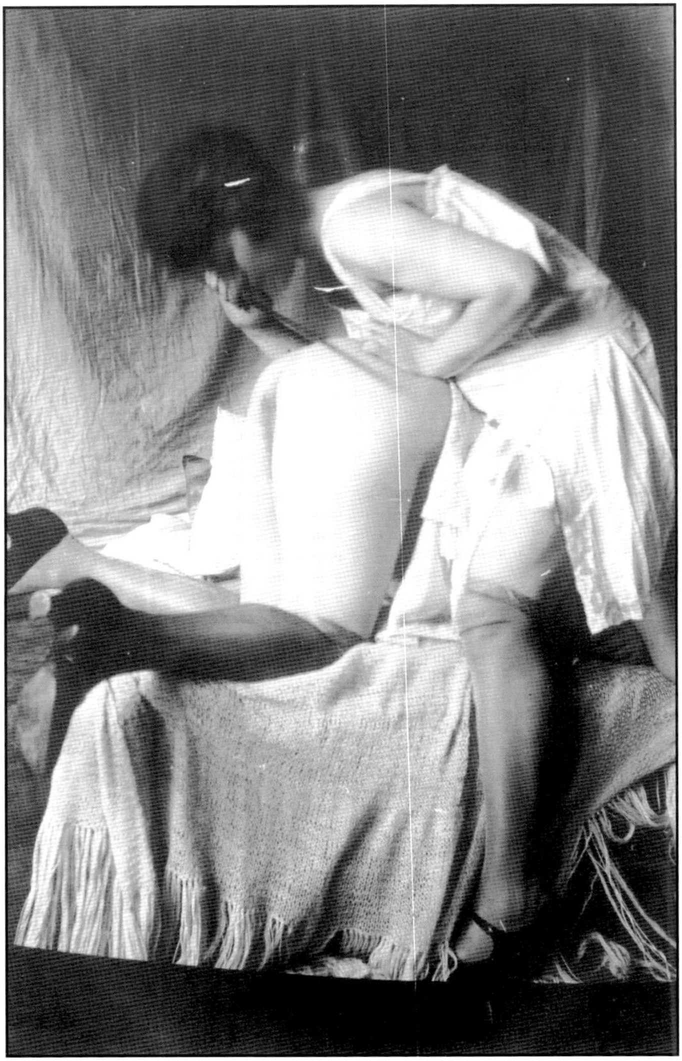

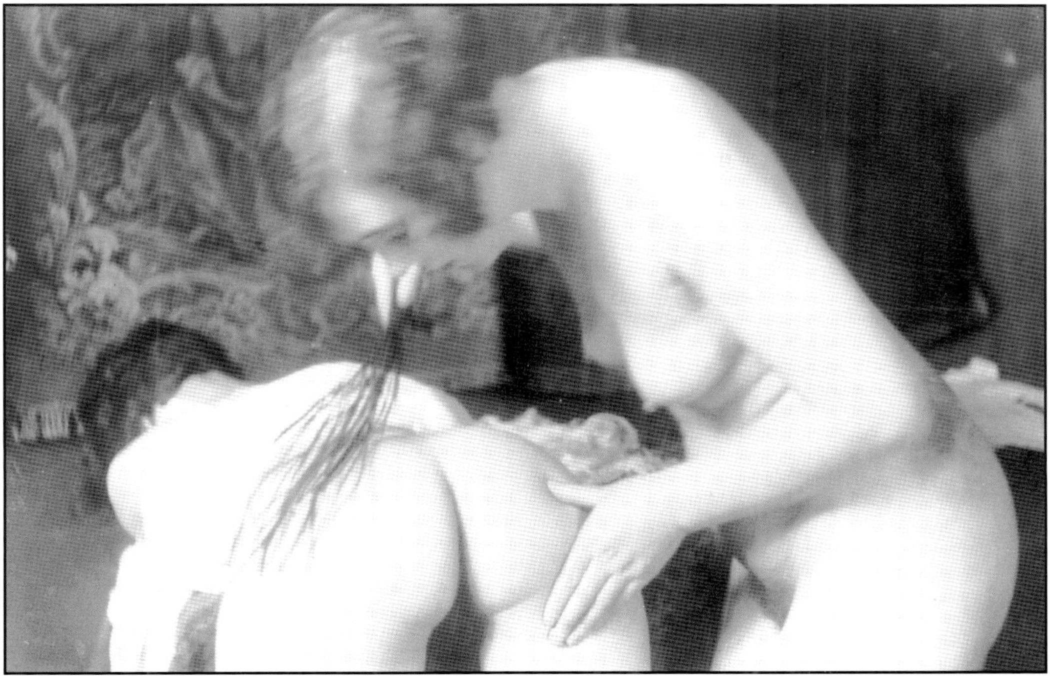

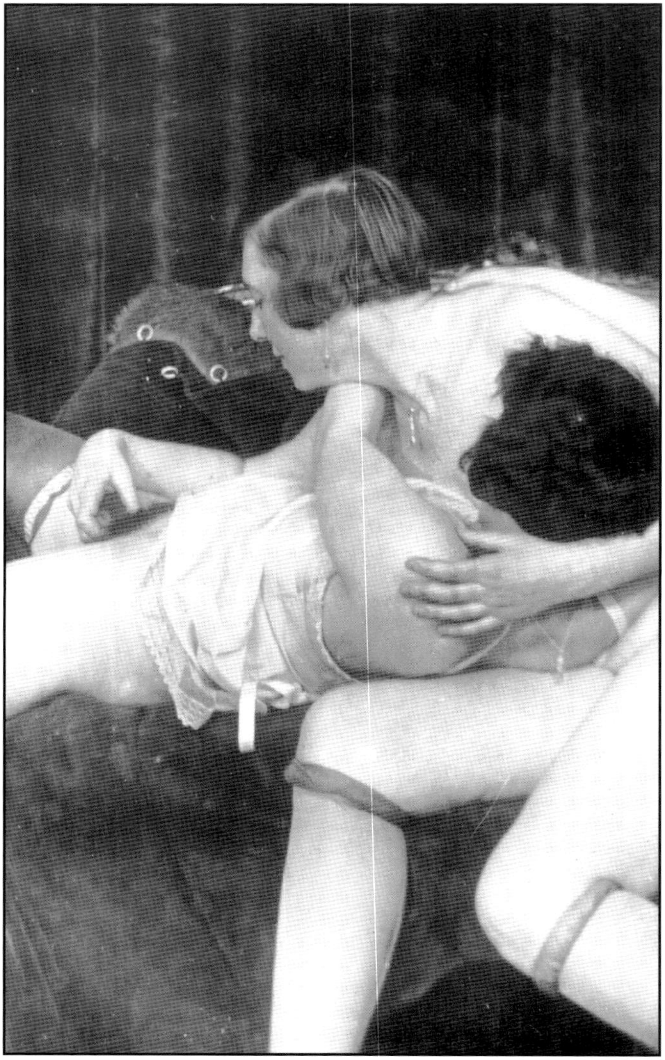

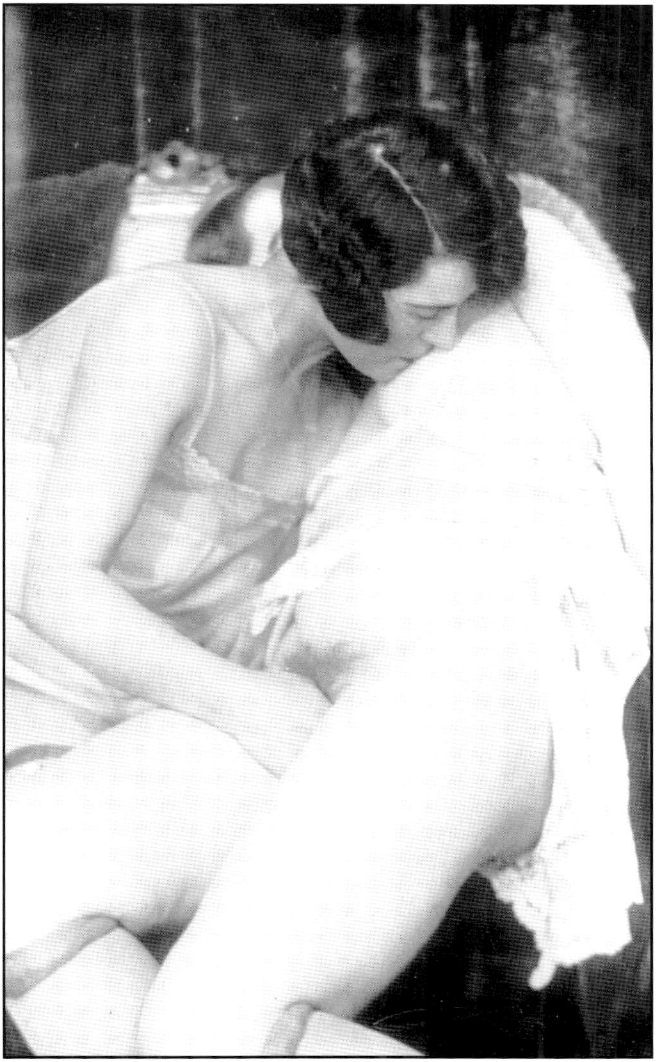

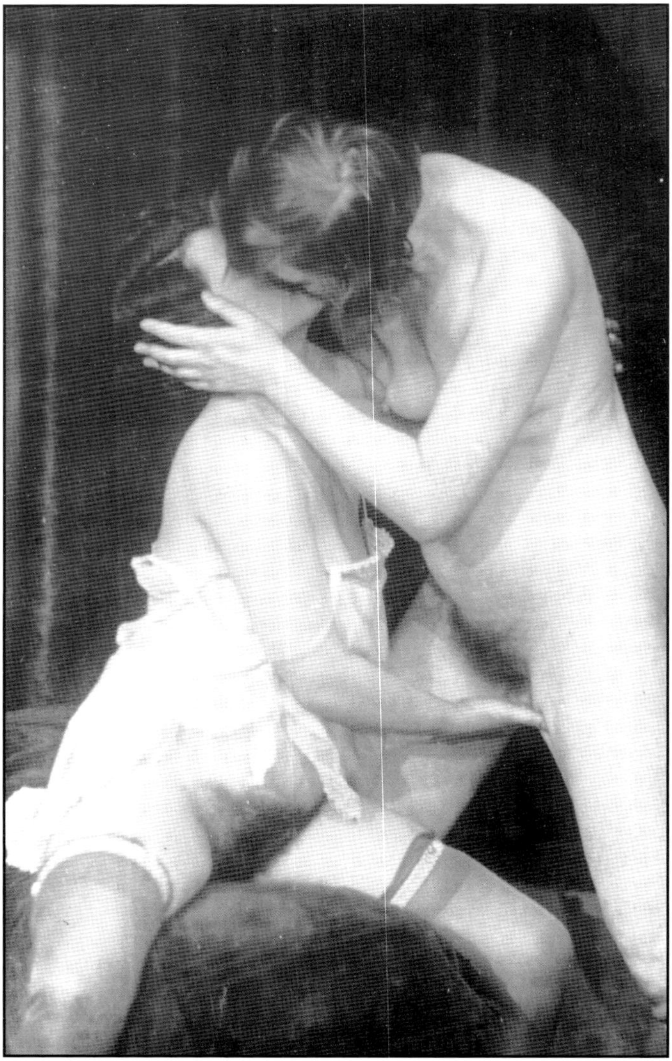

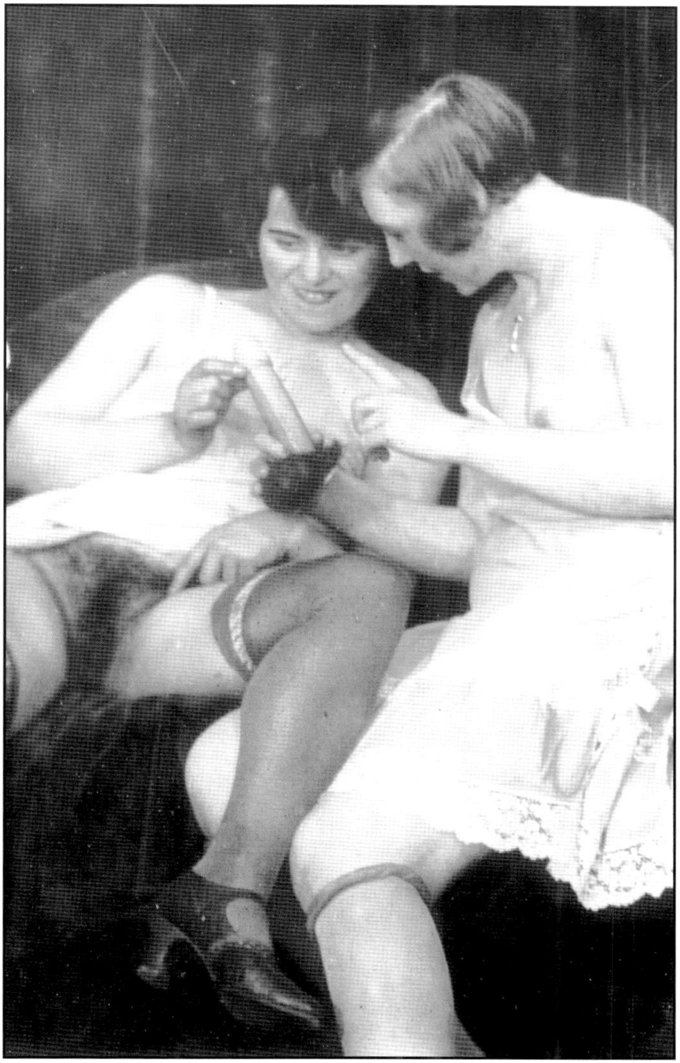

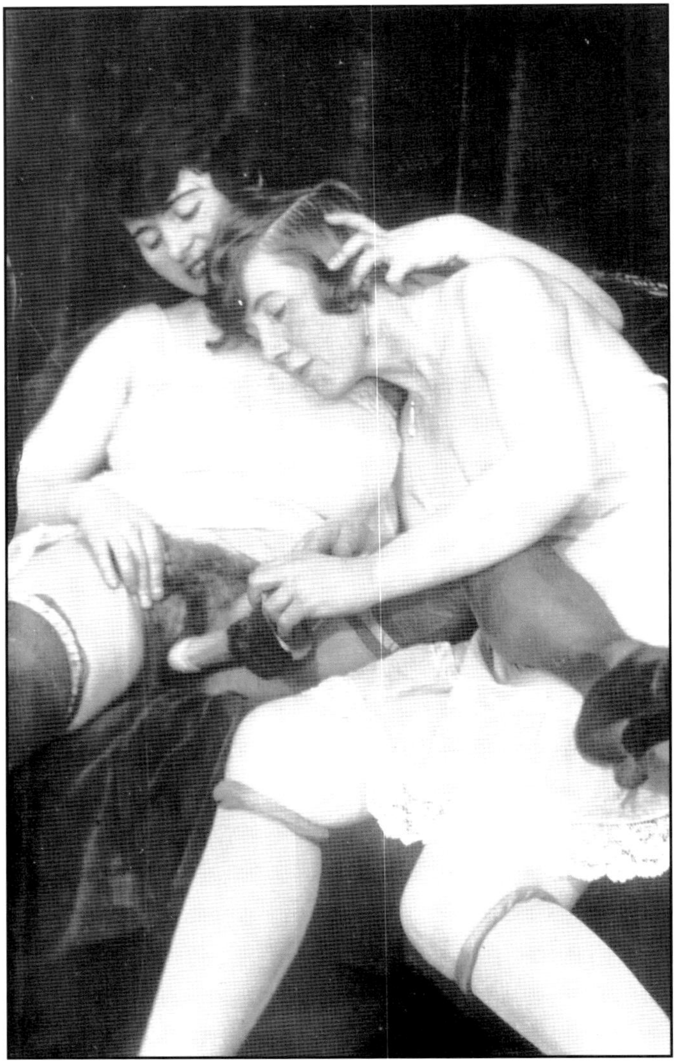

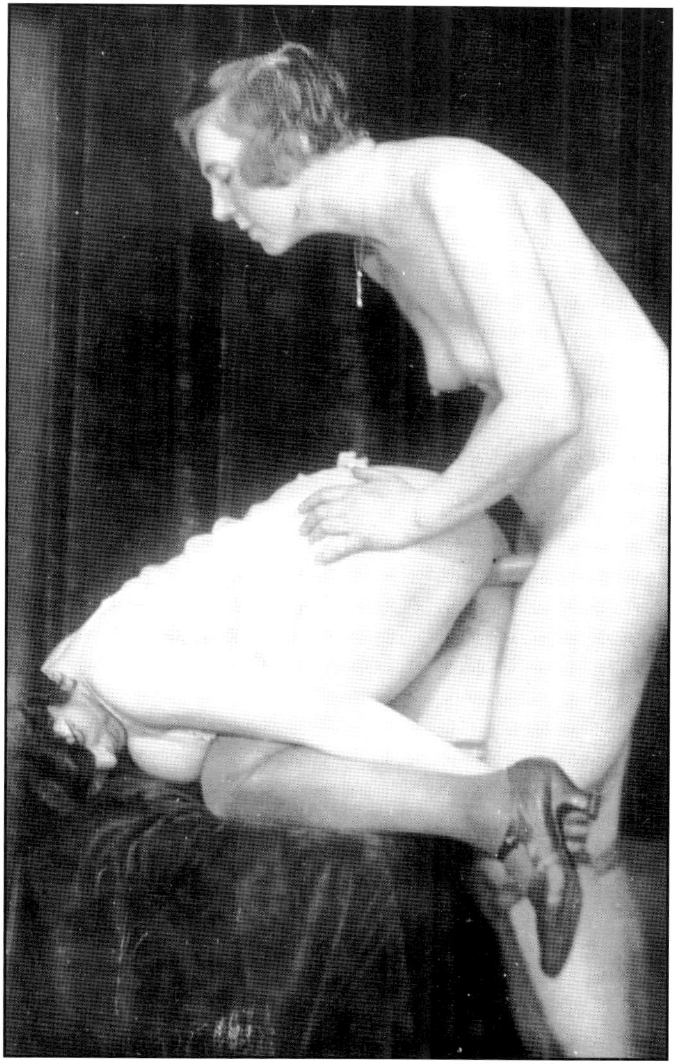

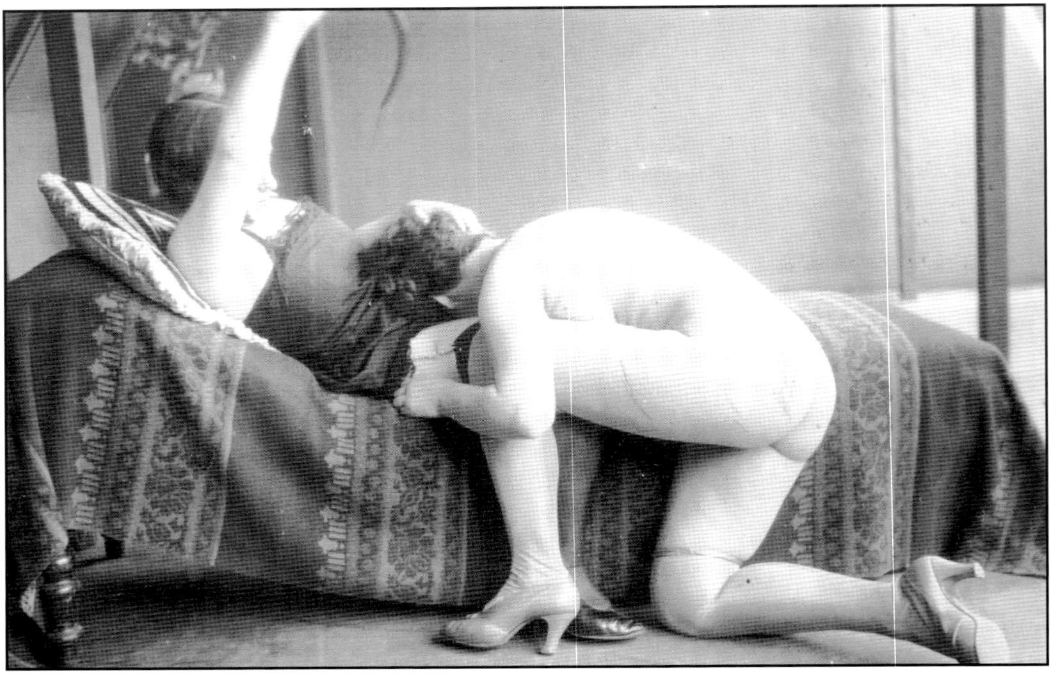

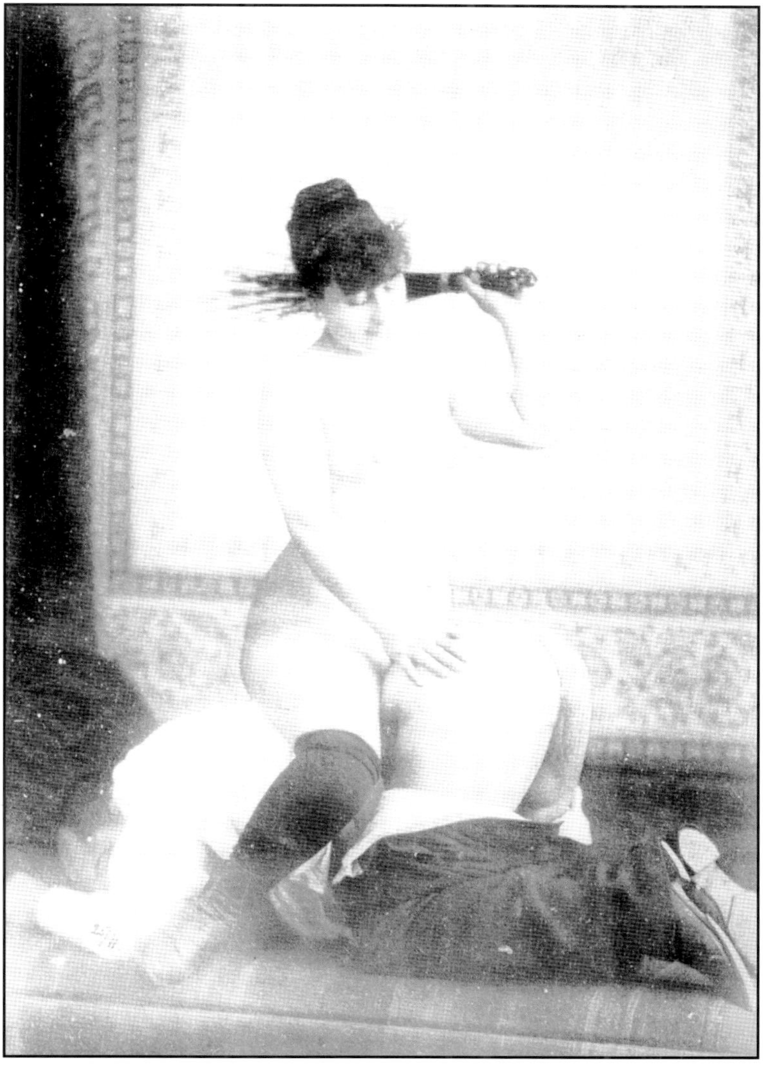

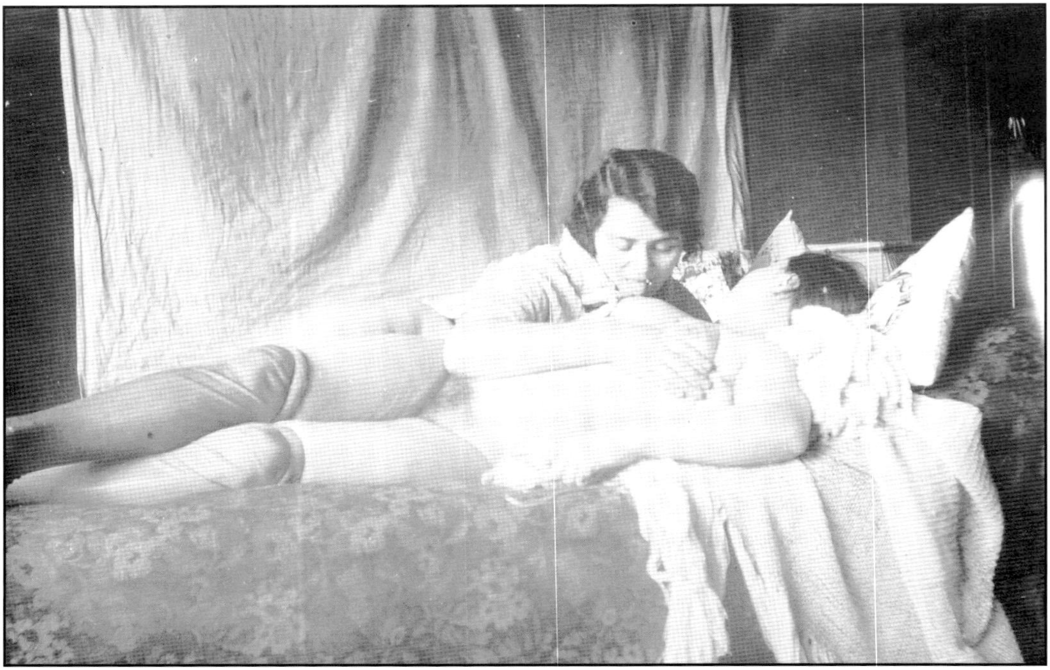

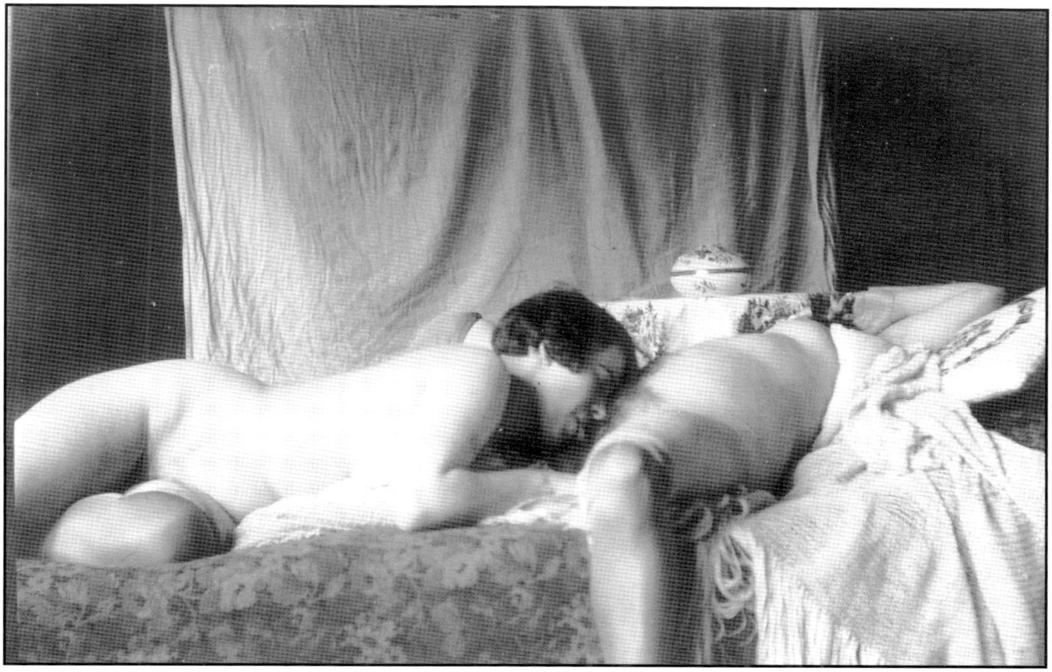

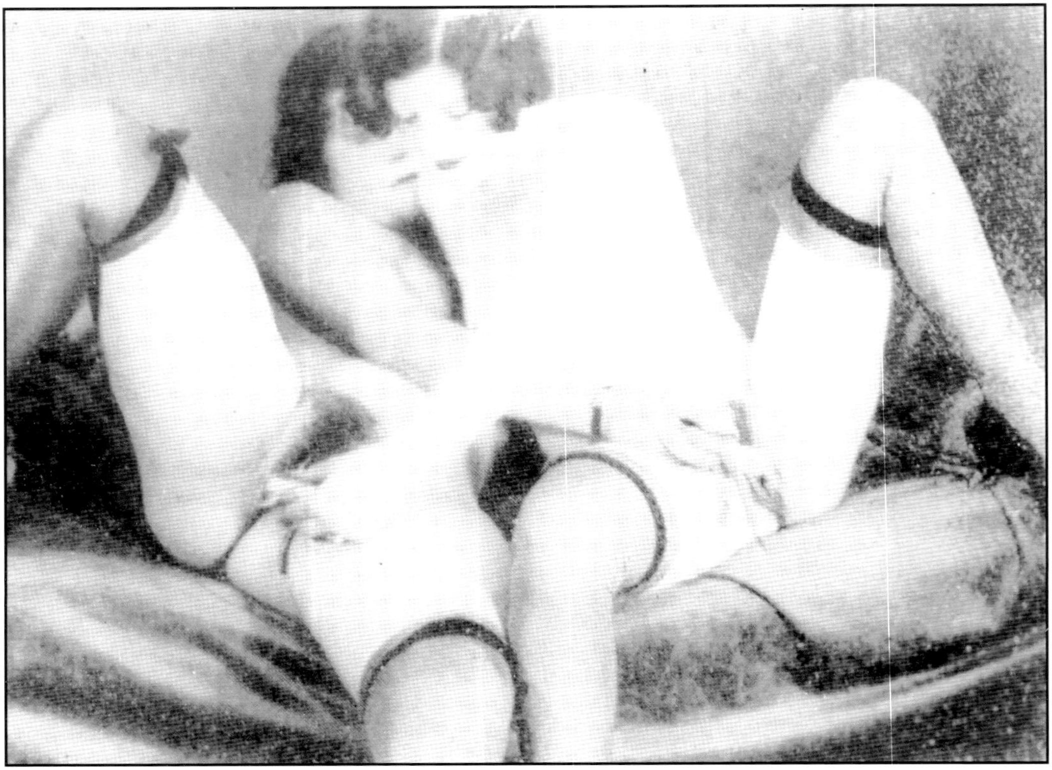

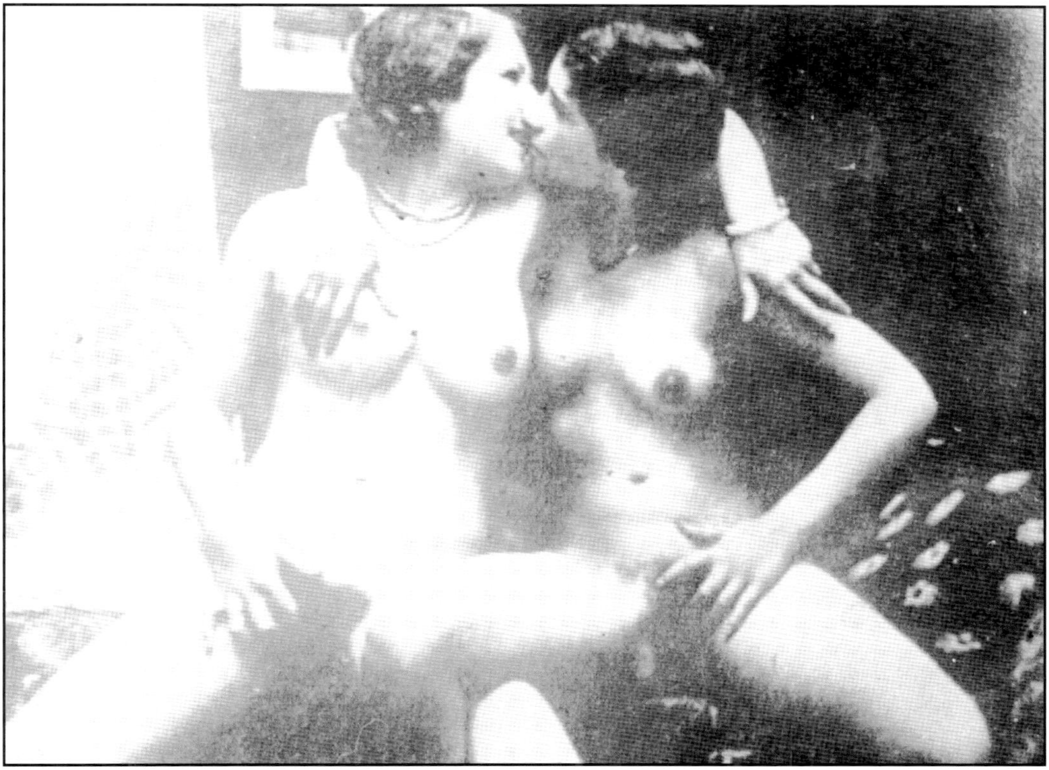

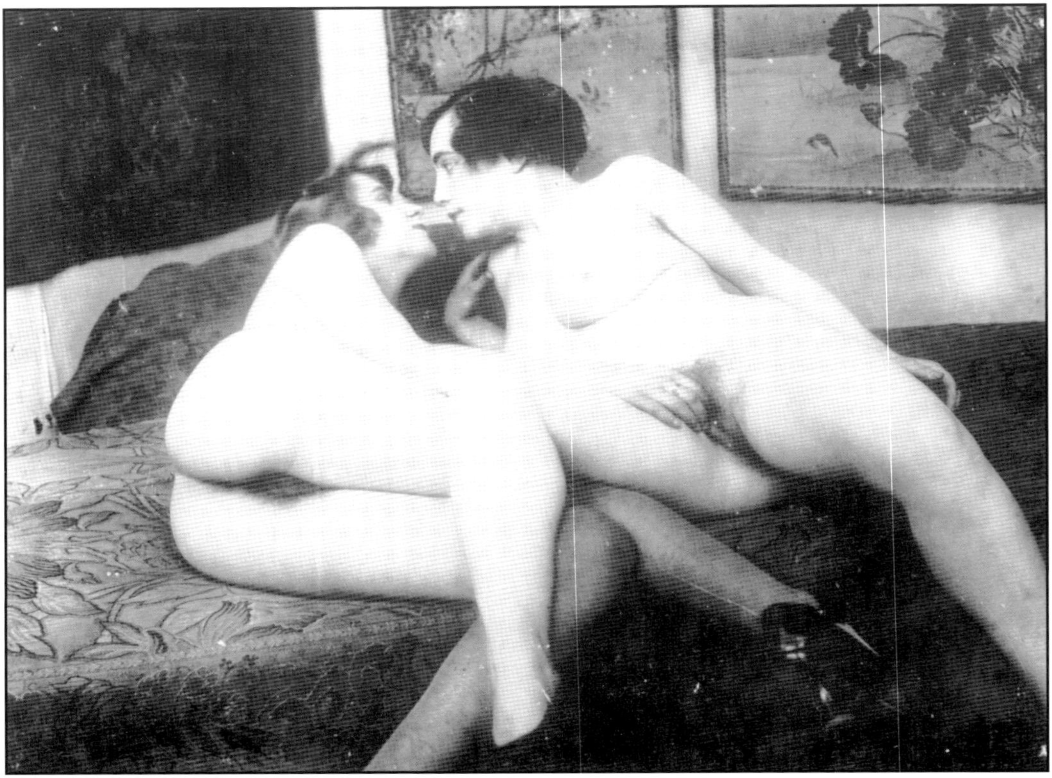

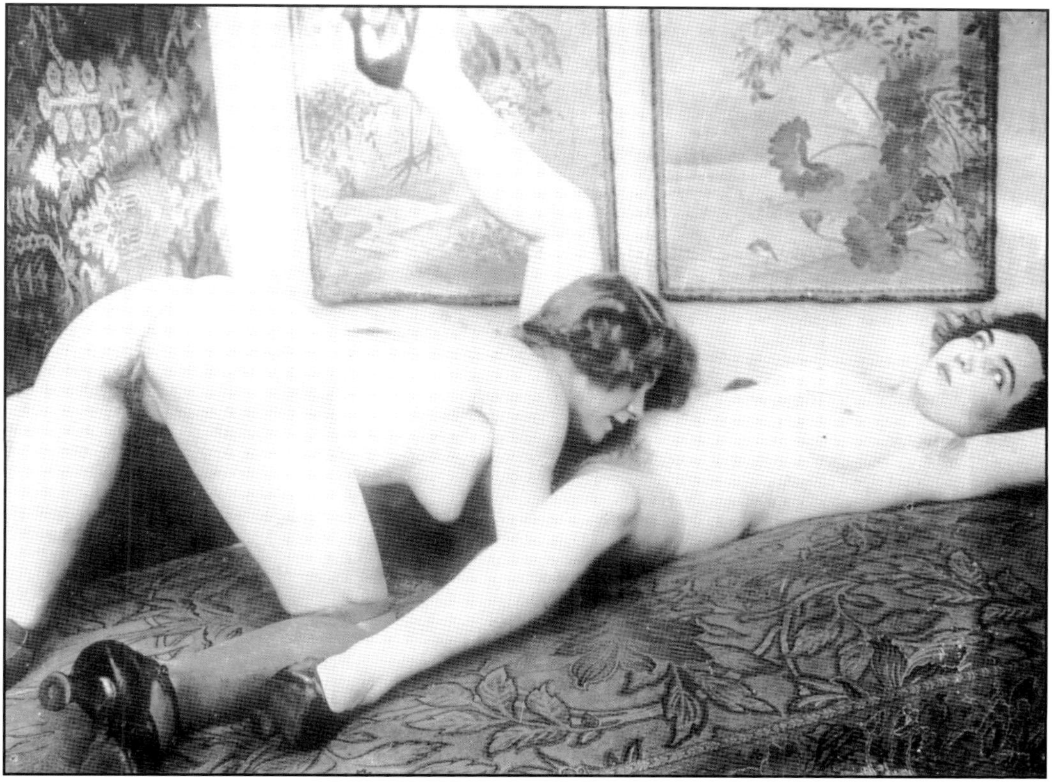

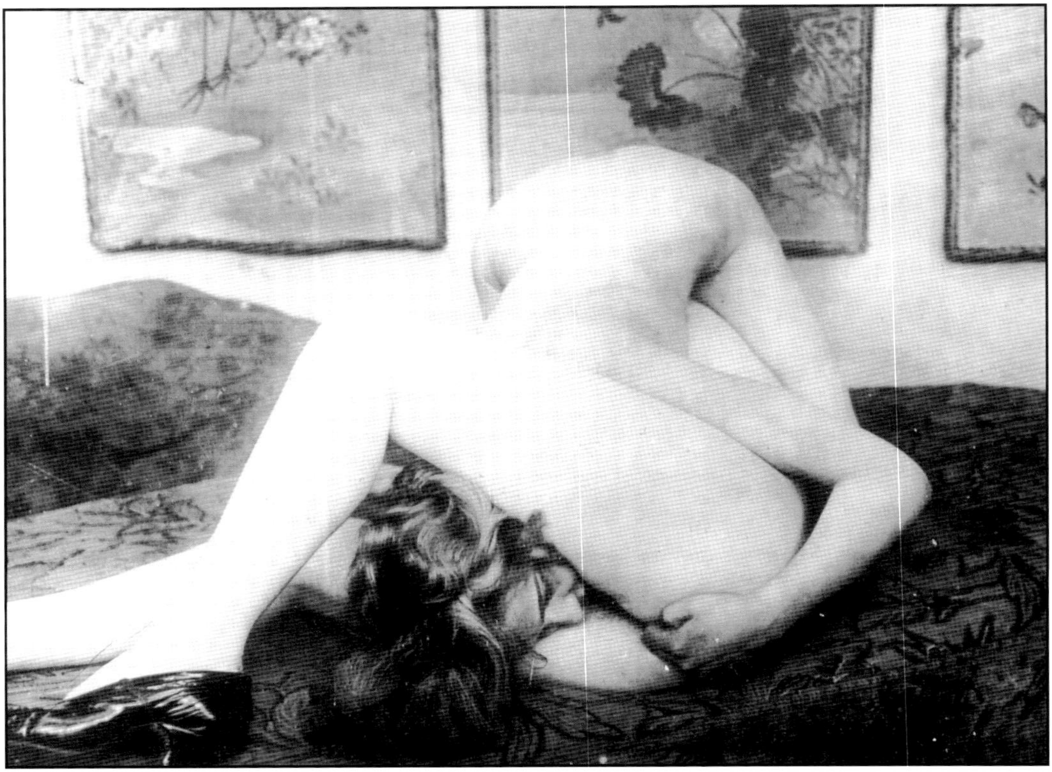

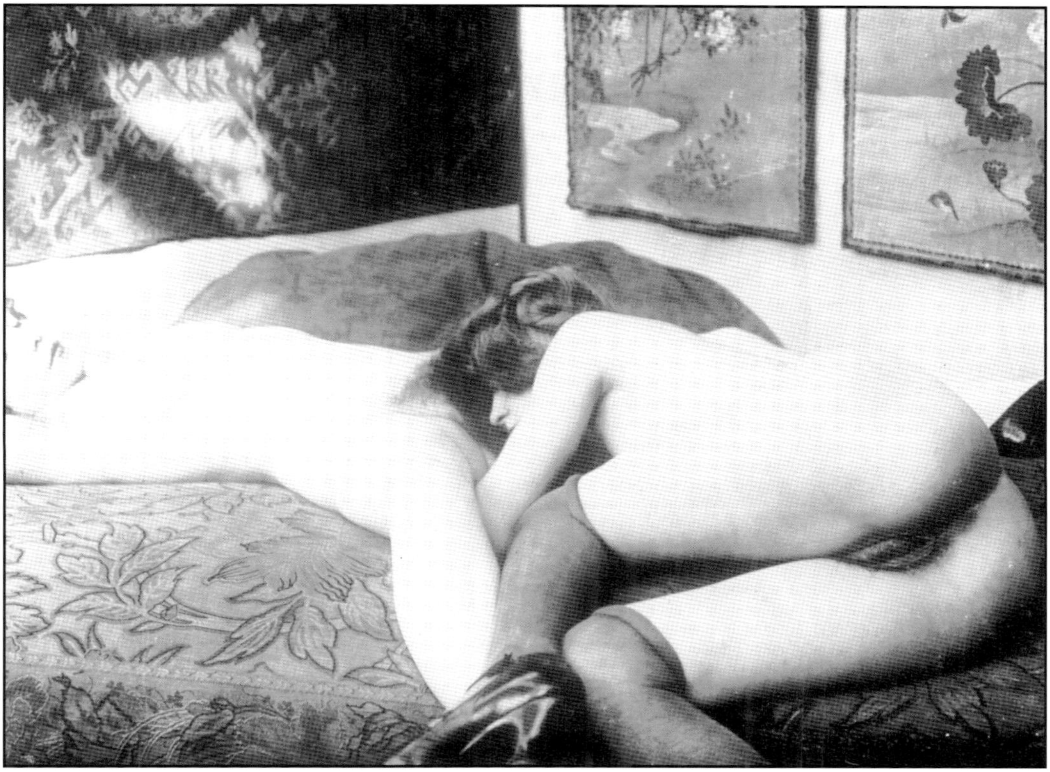

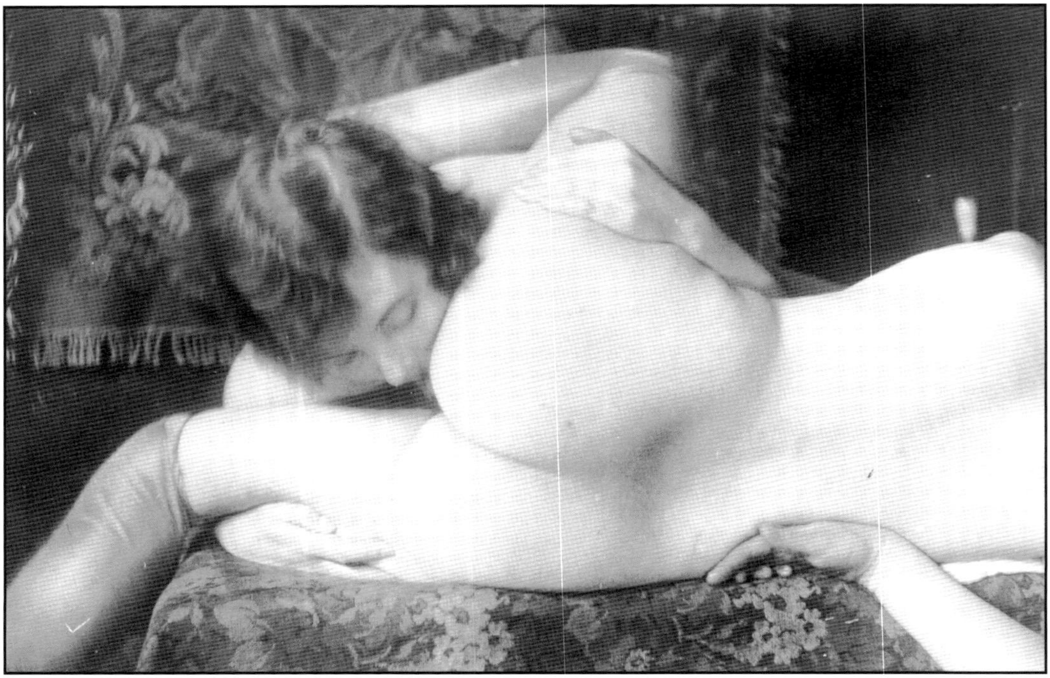

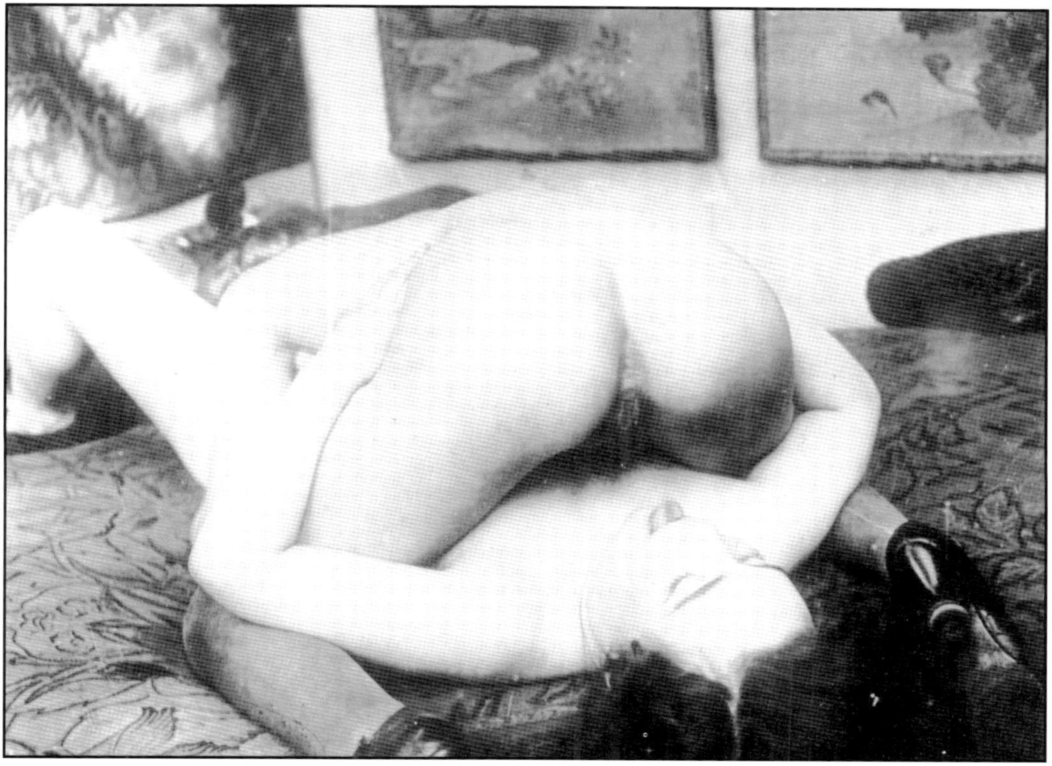

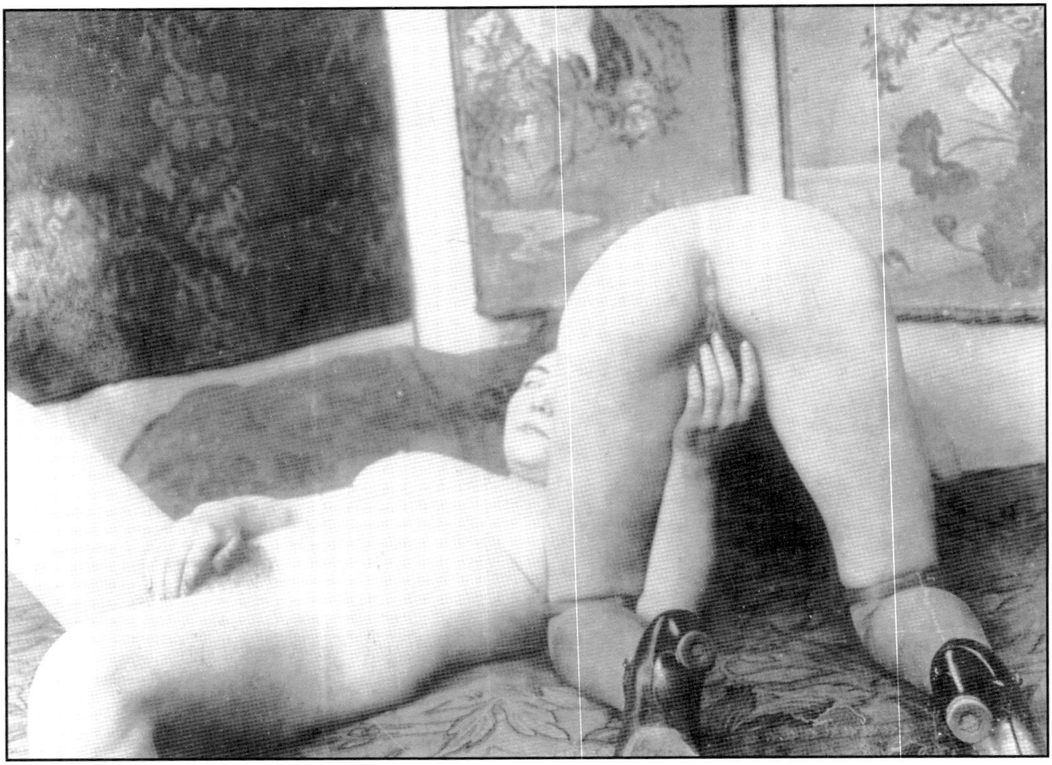

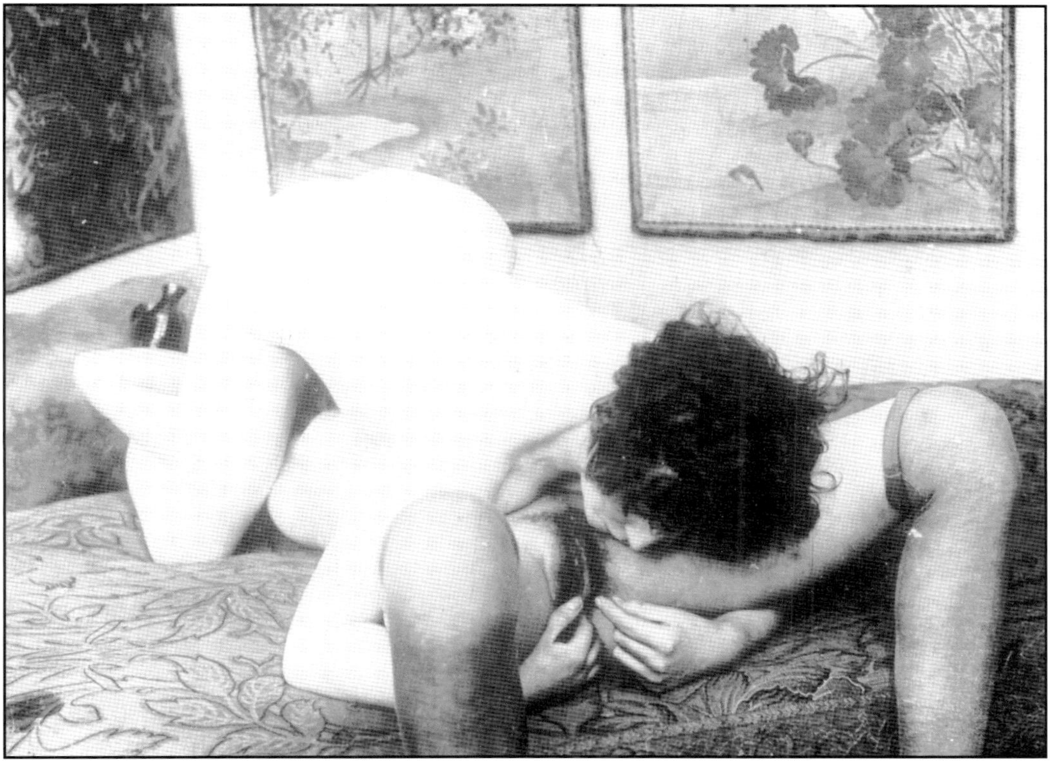

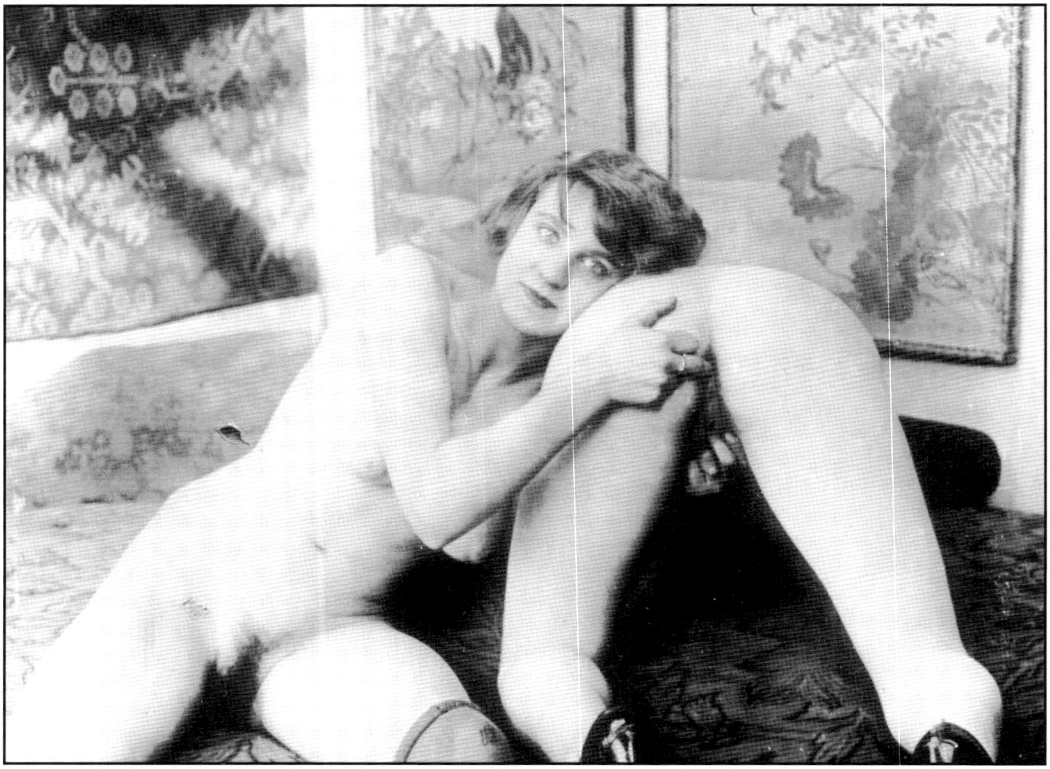

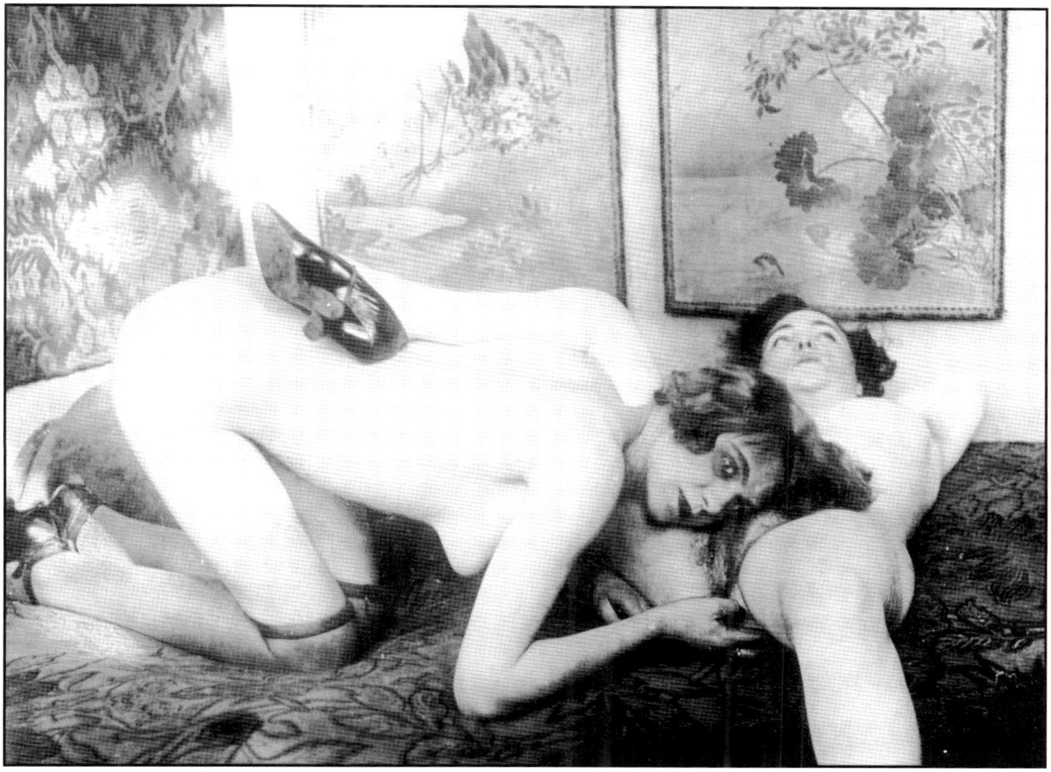

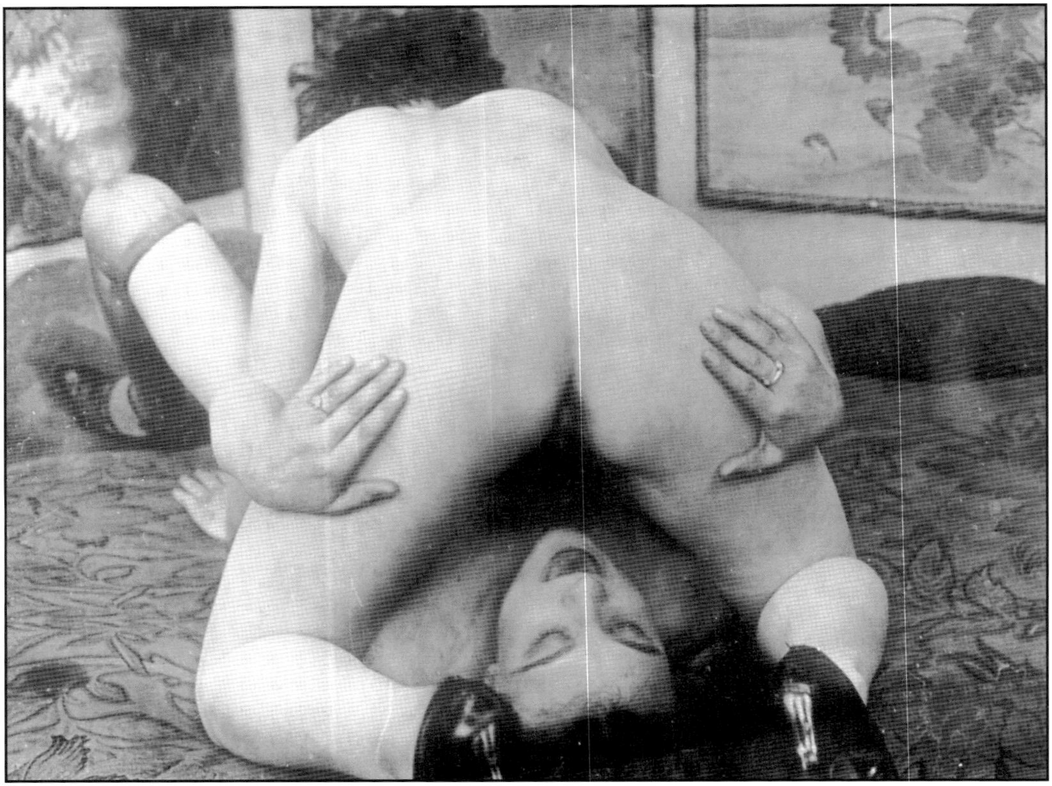

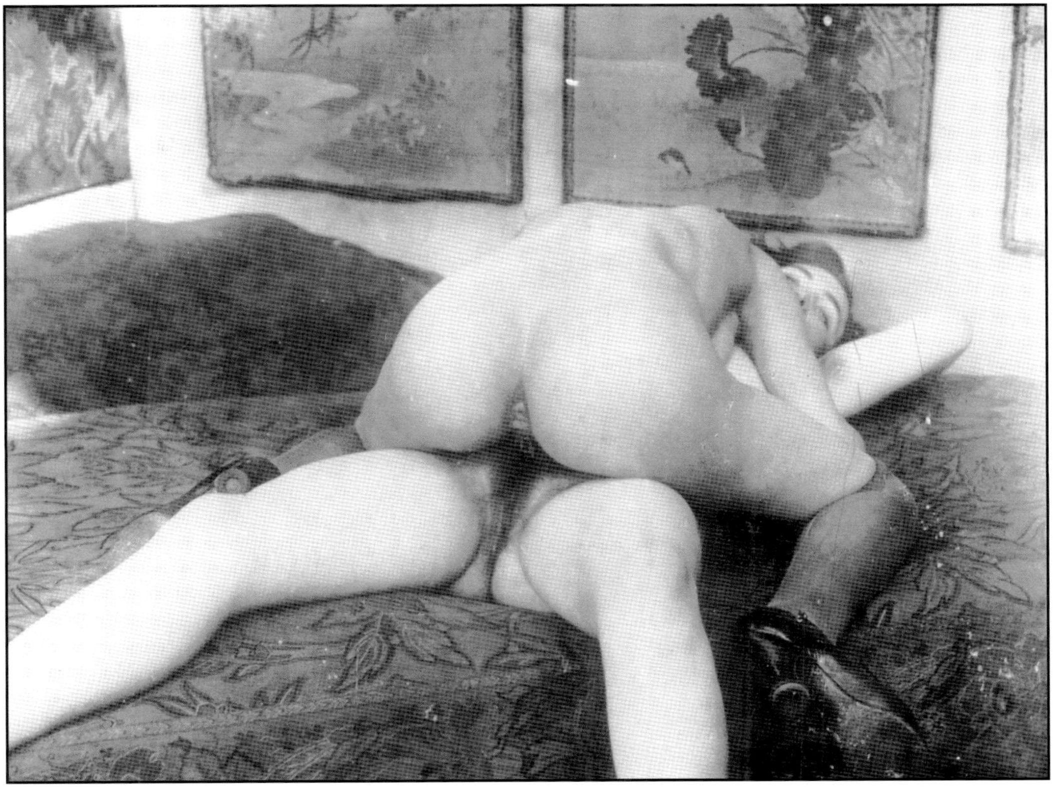

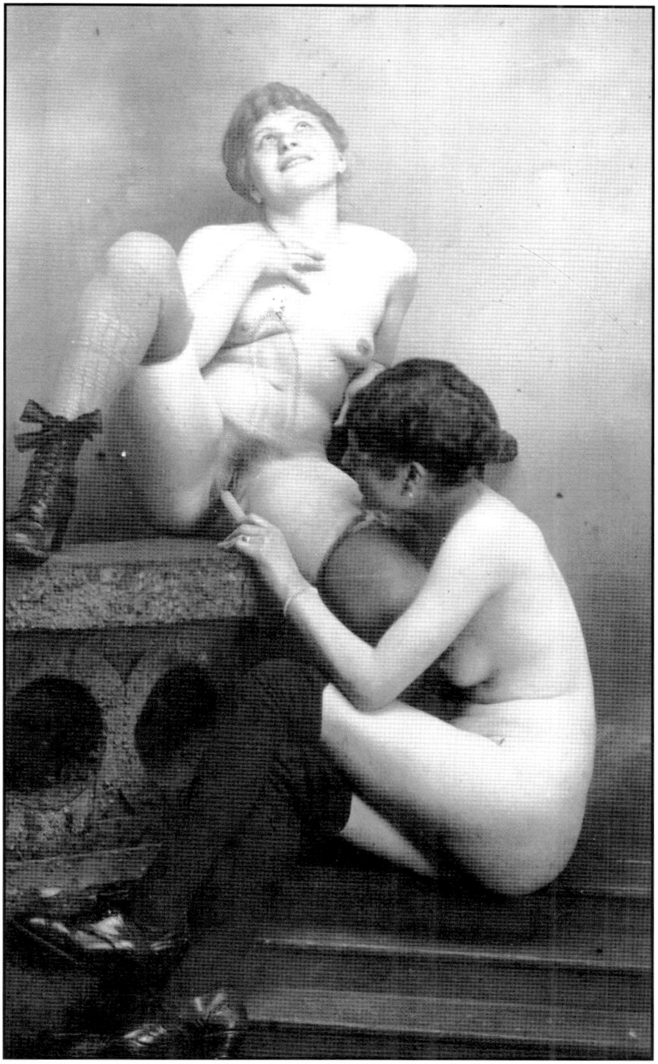

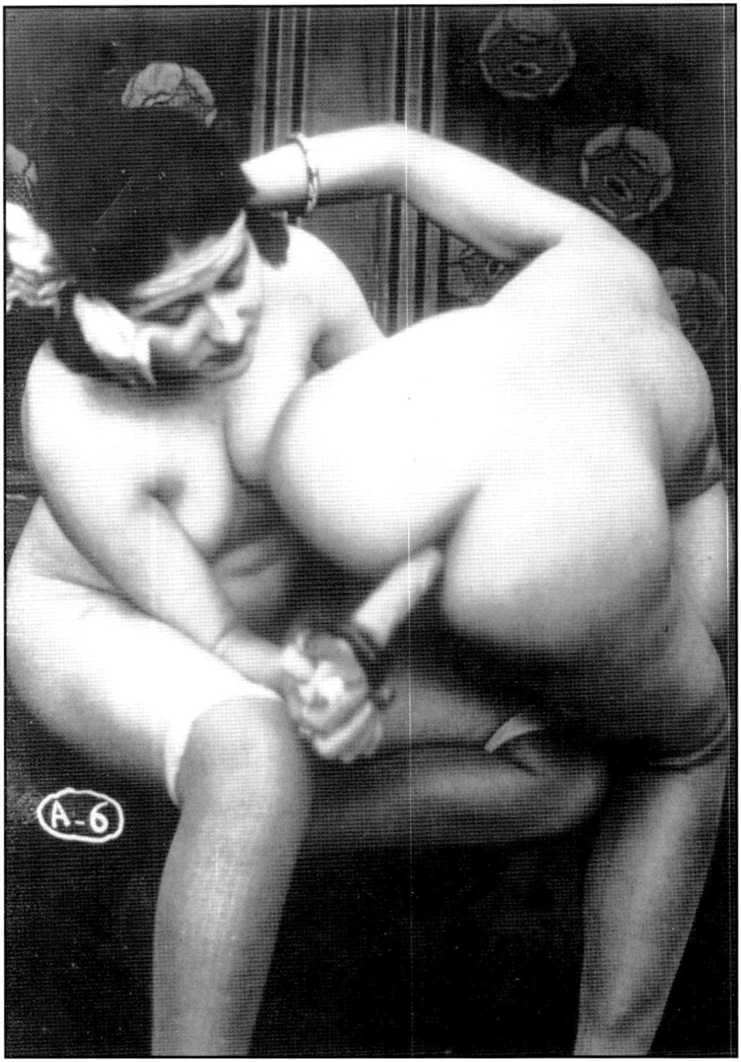
A-6

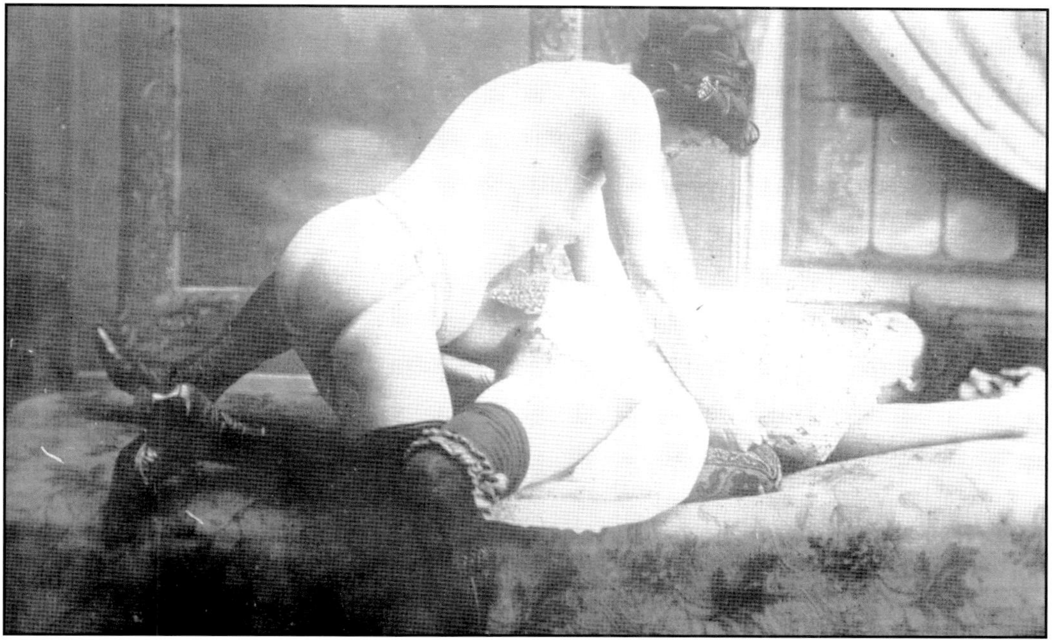

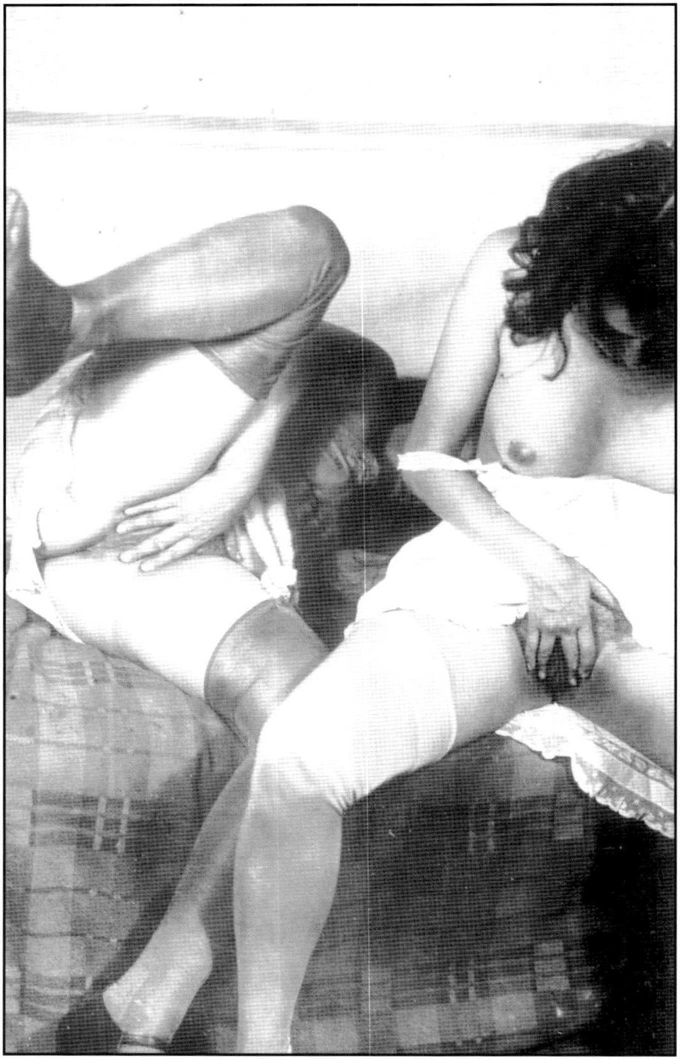

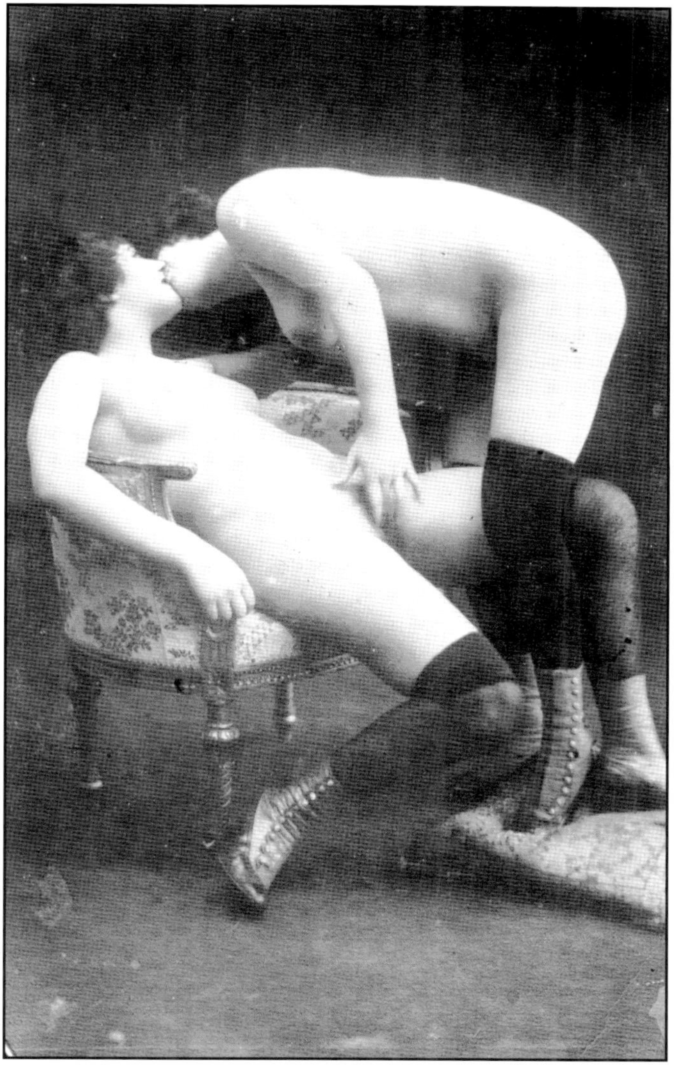

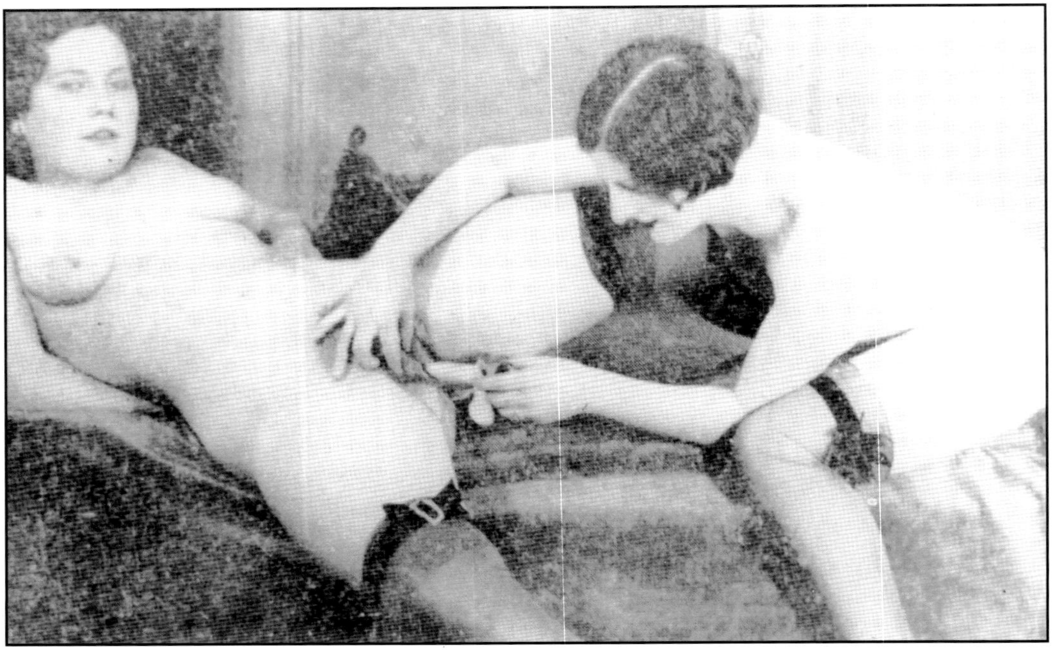

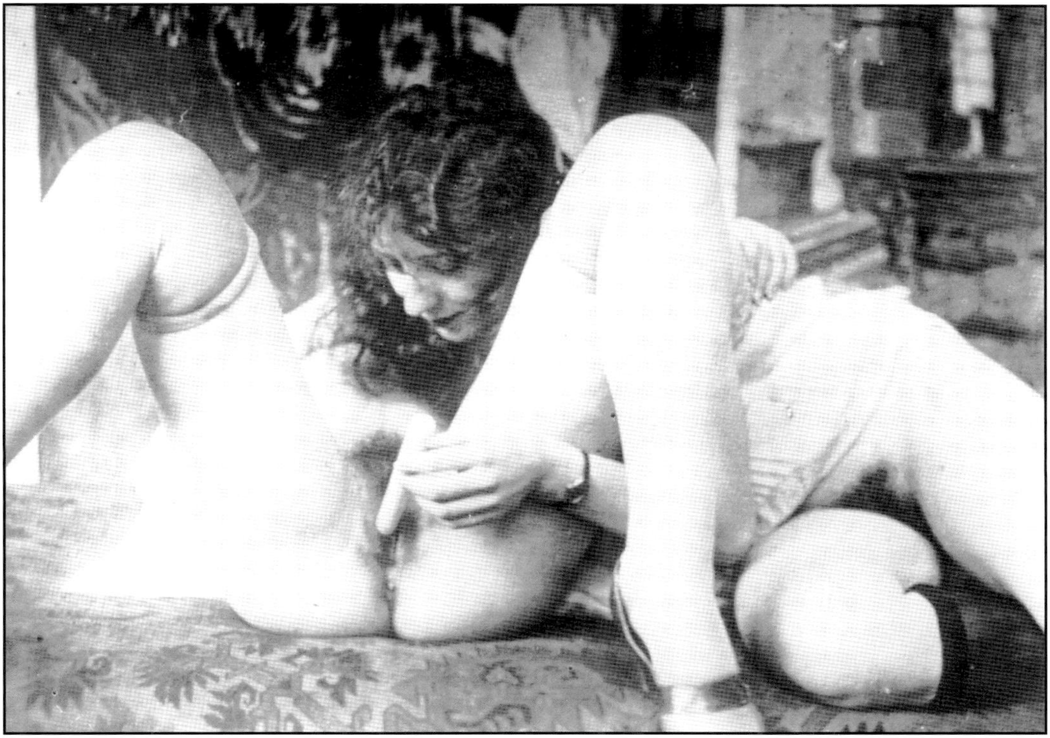

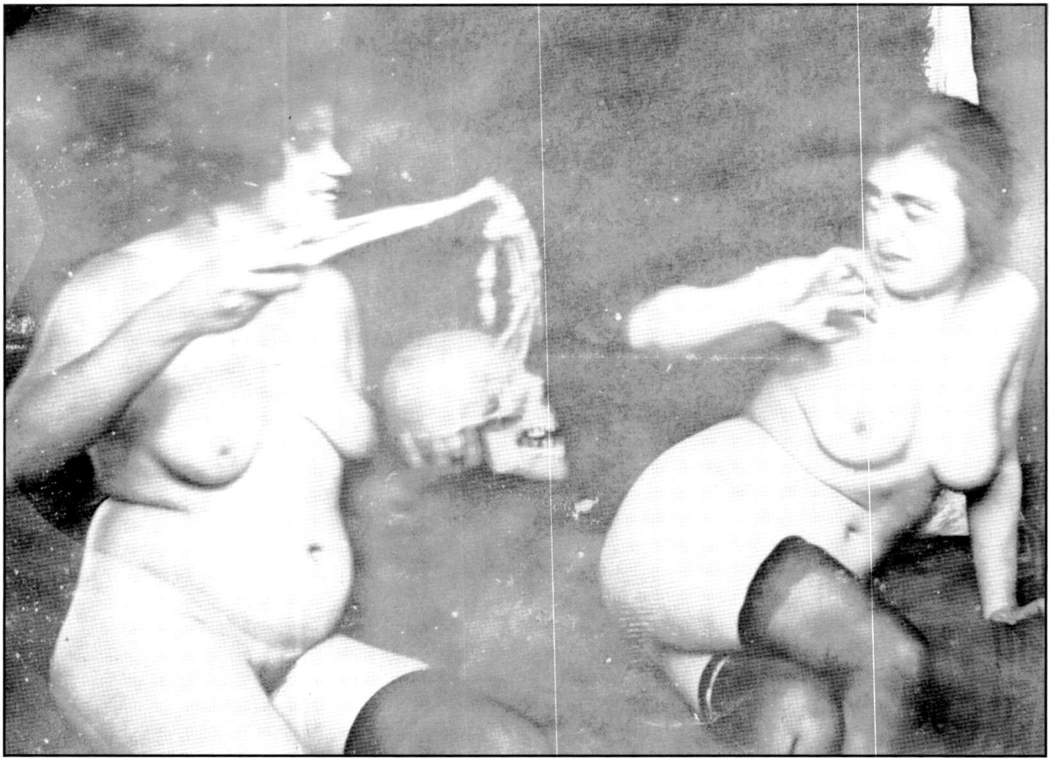

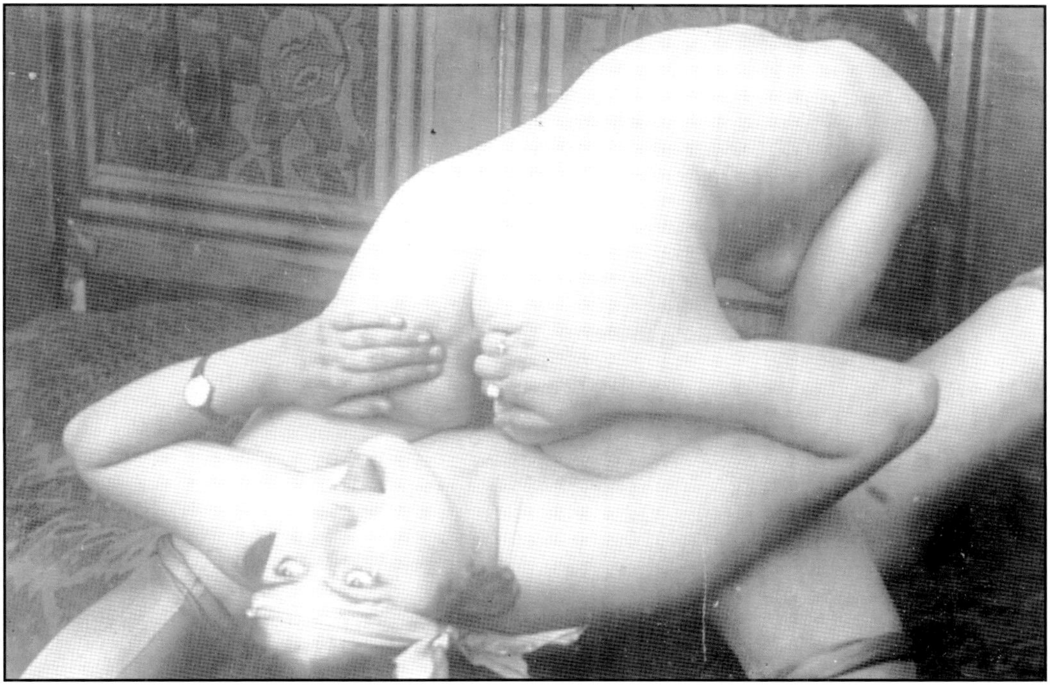

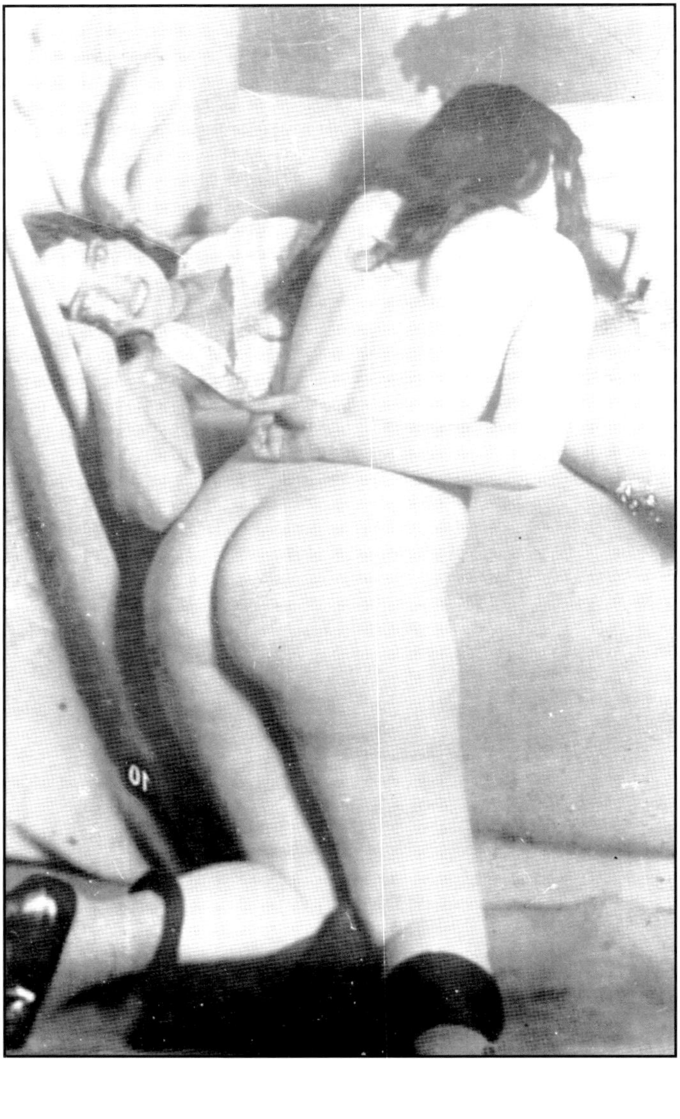

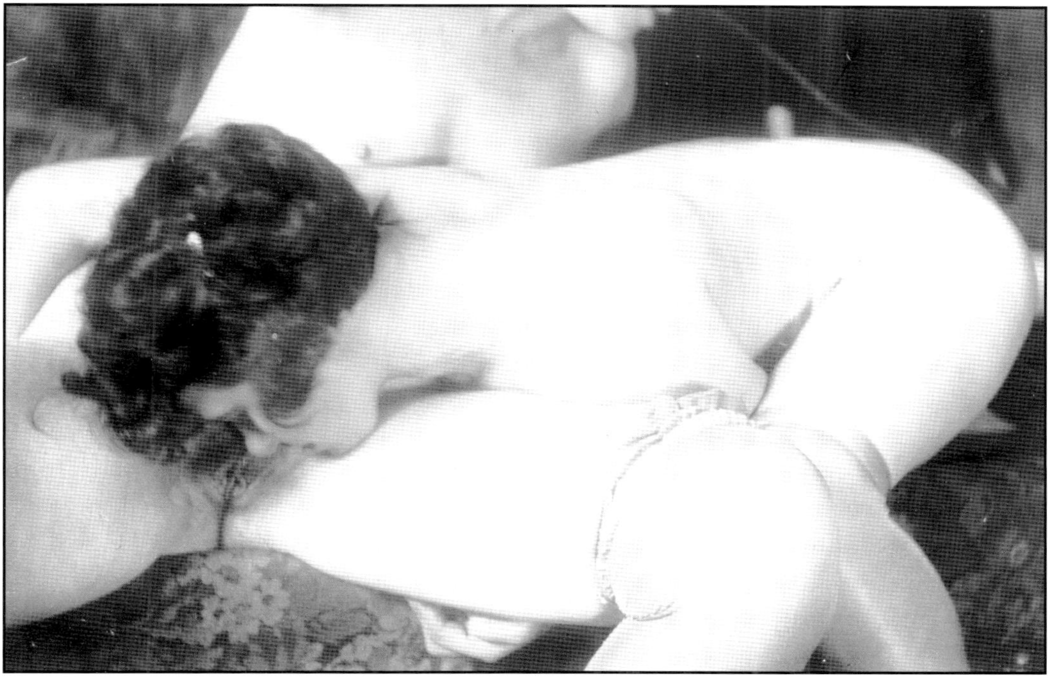

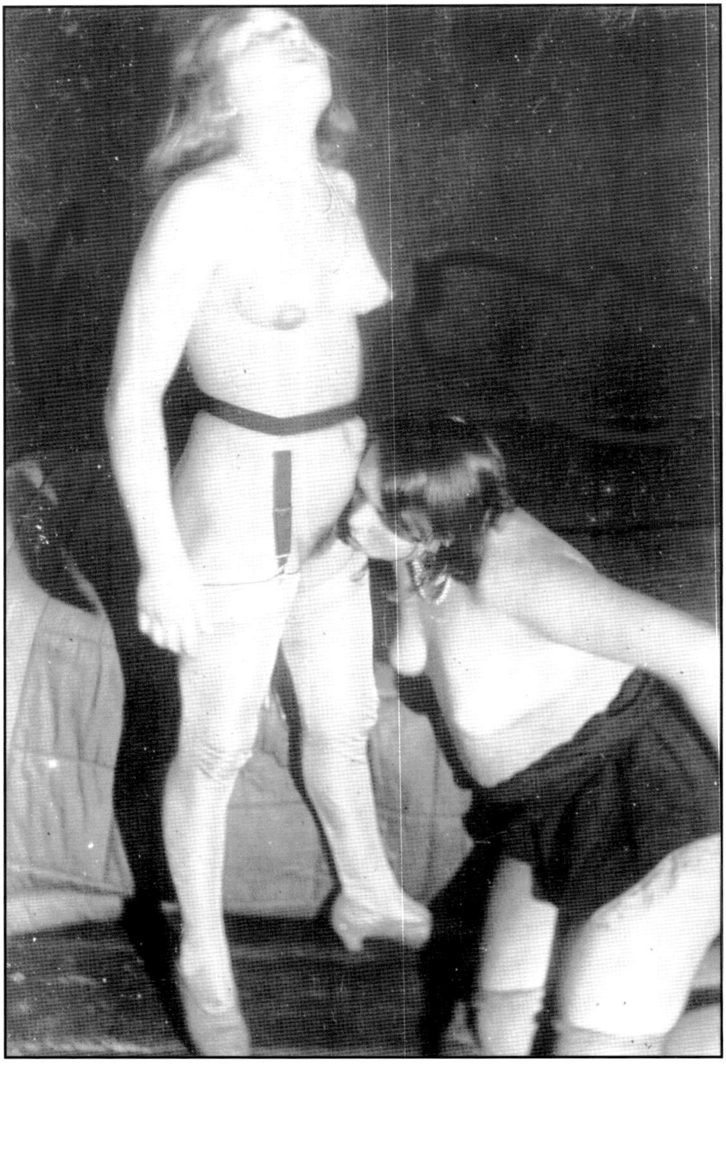

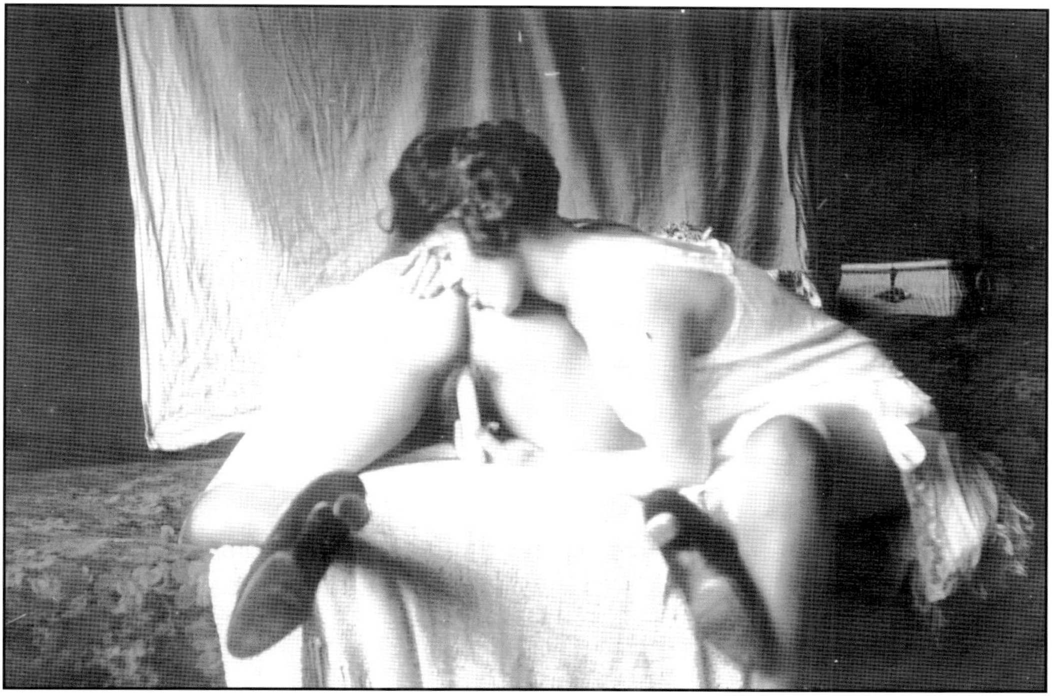

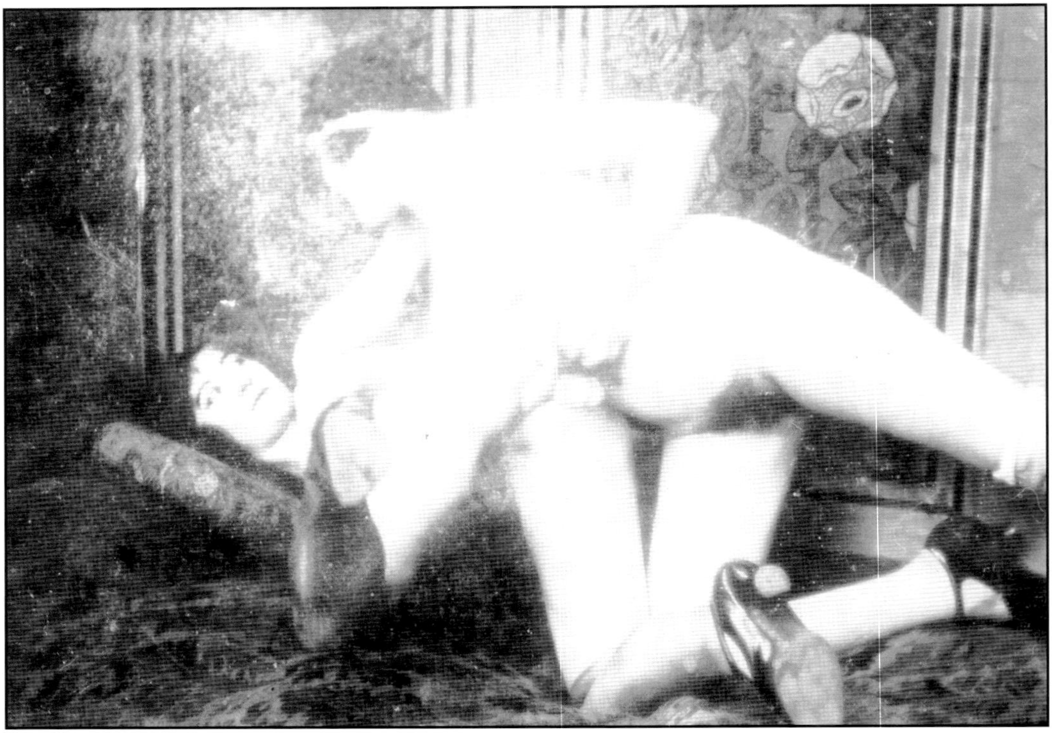

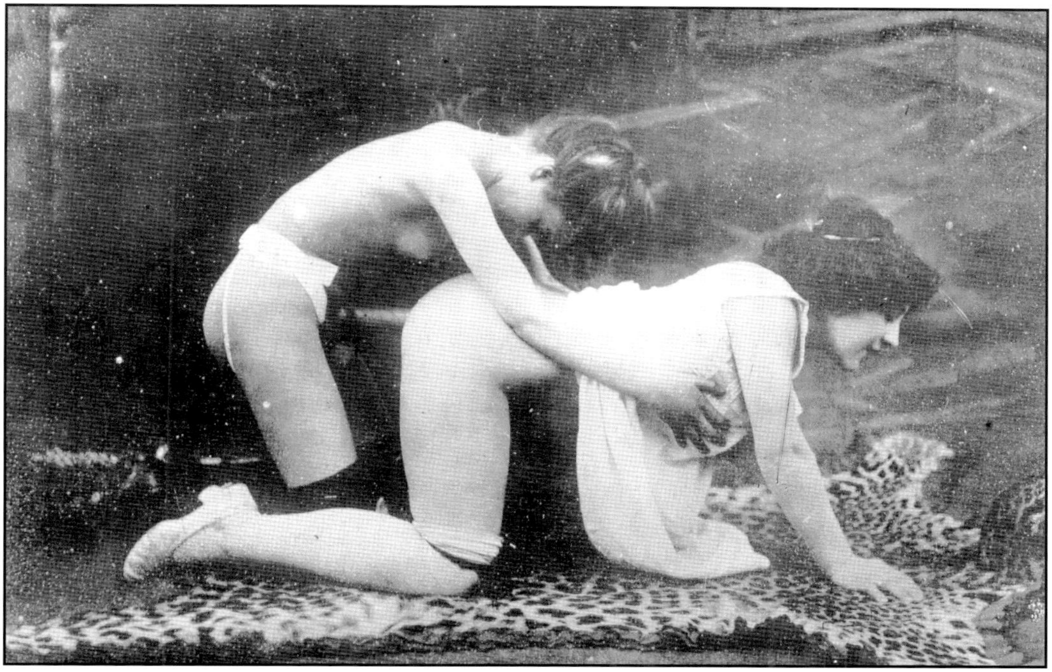

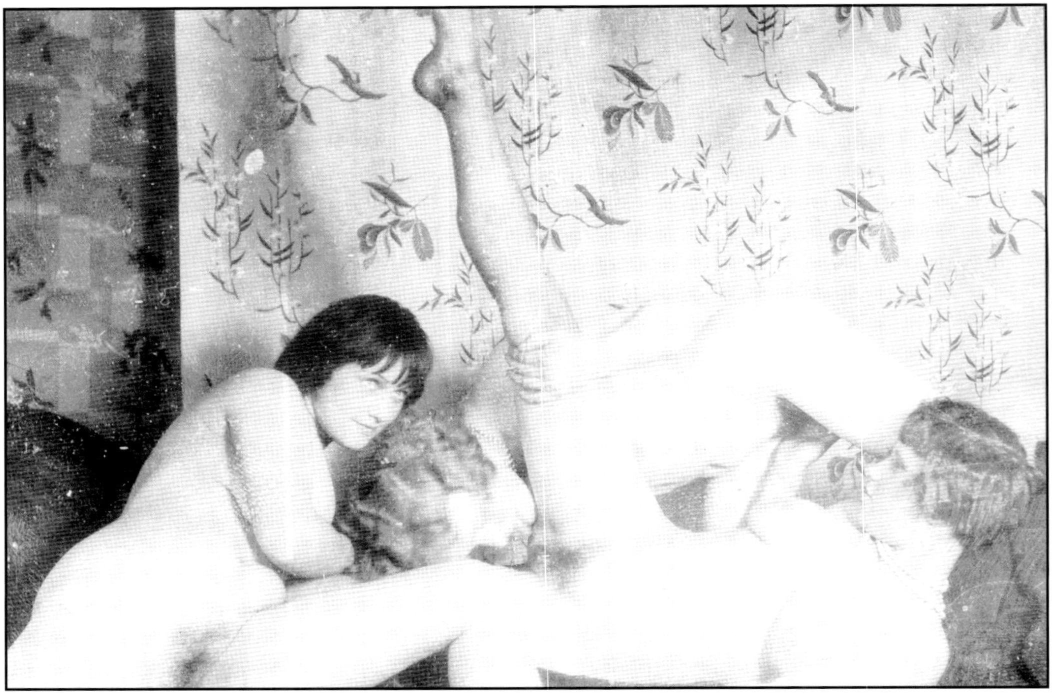

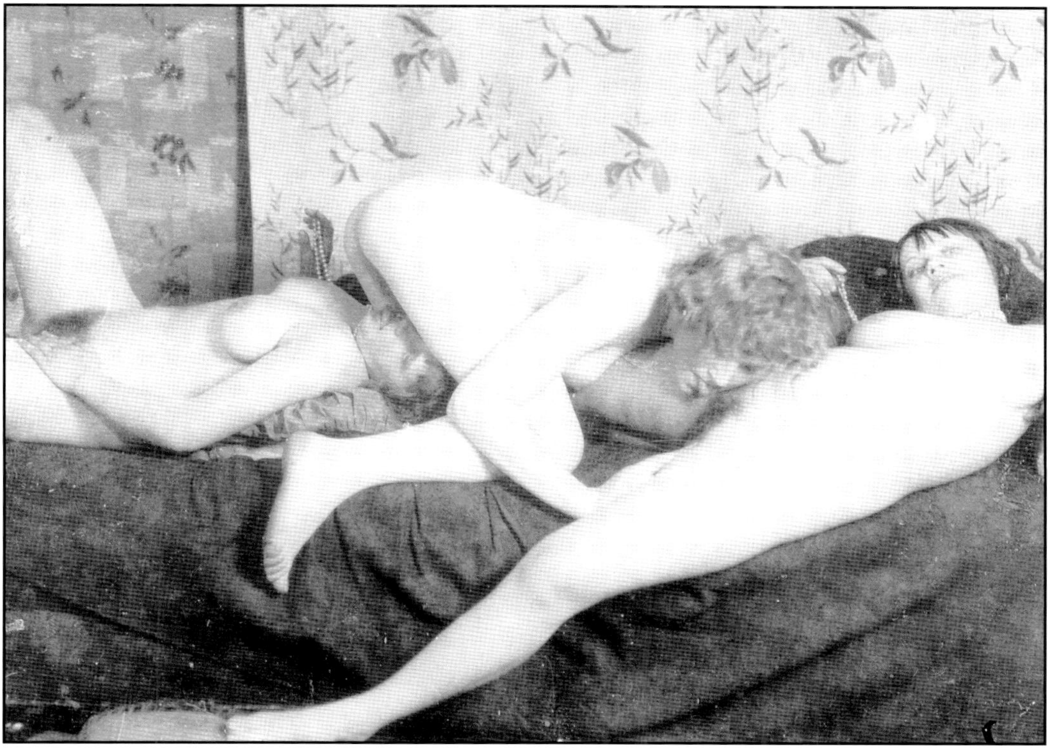

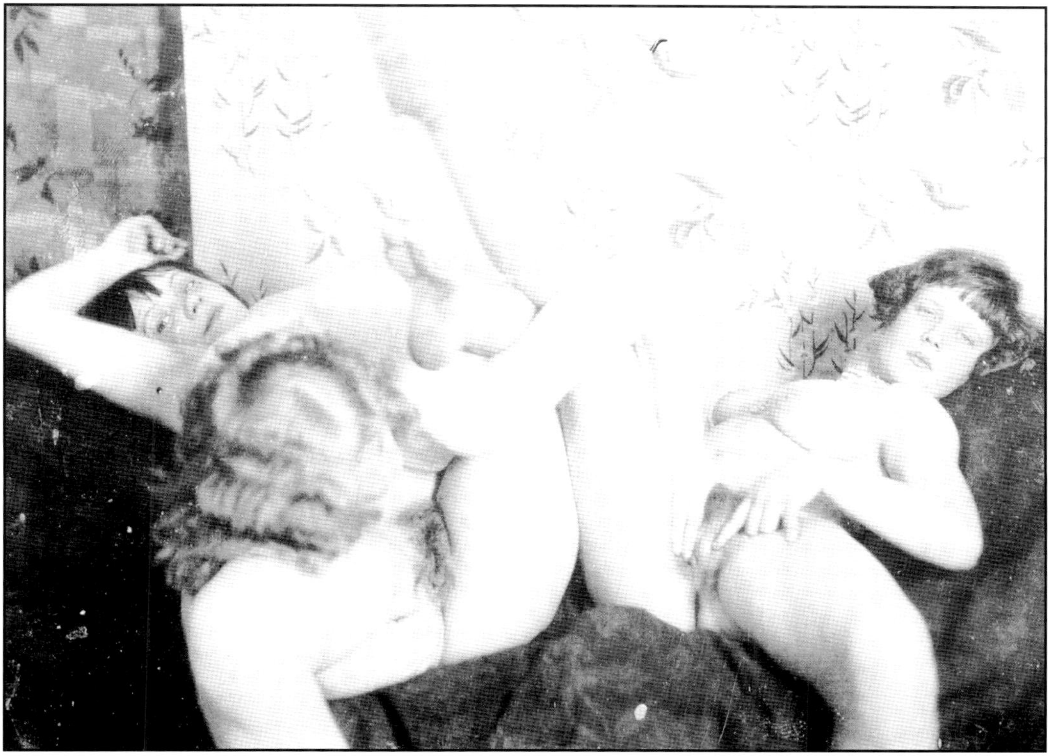

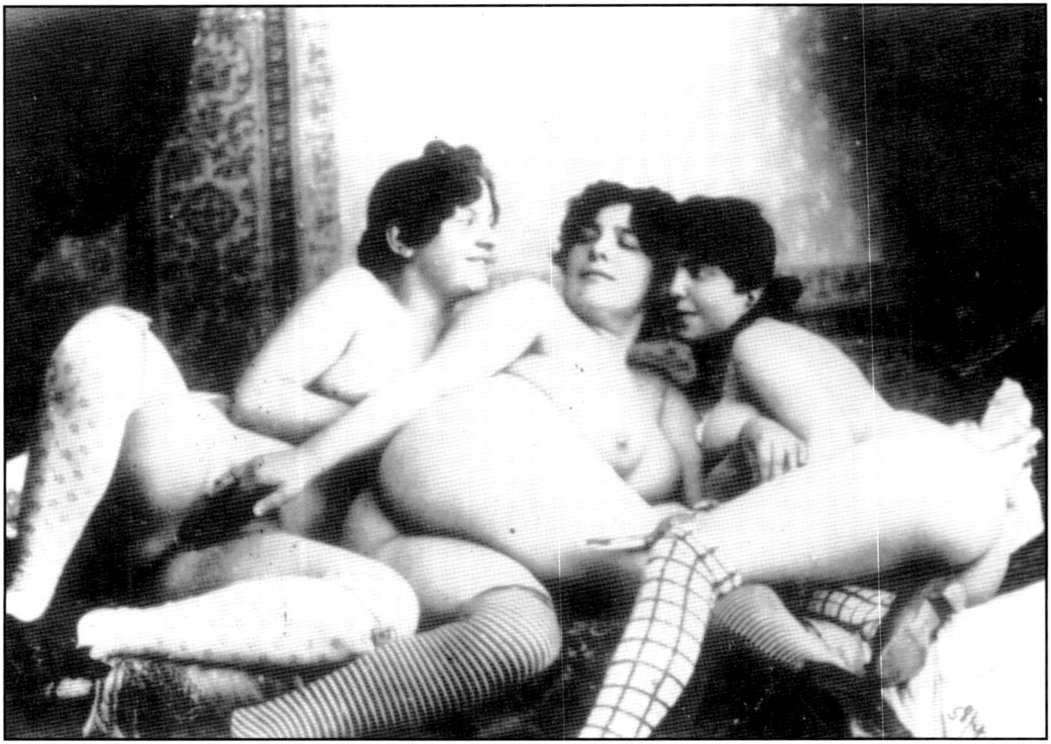

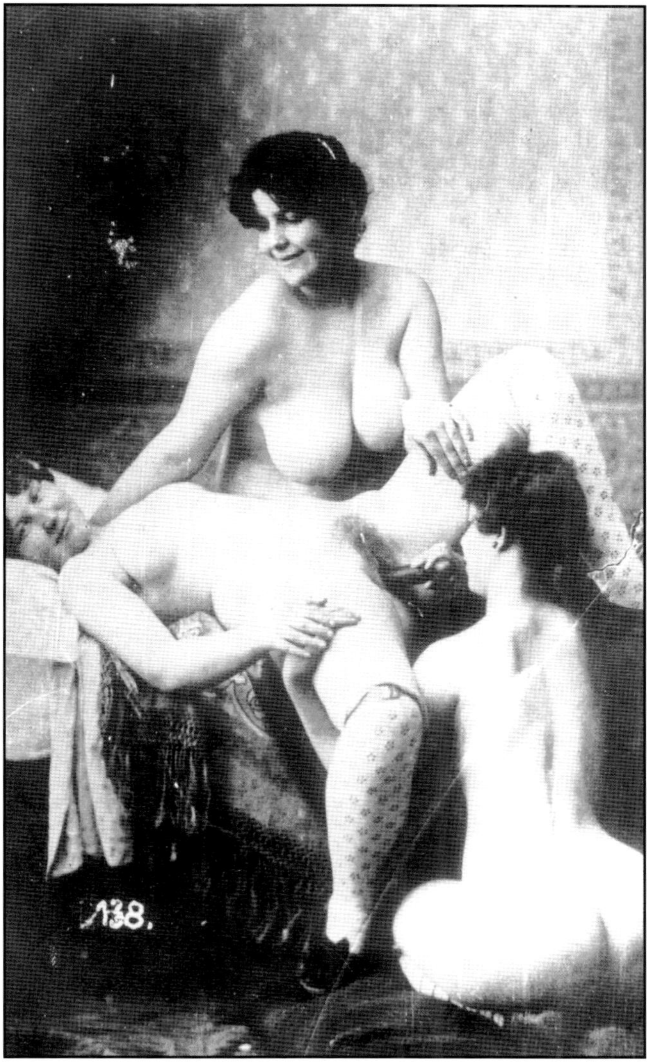
138.

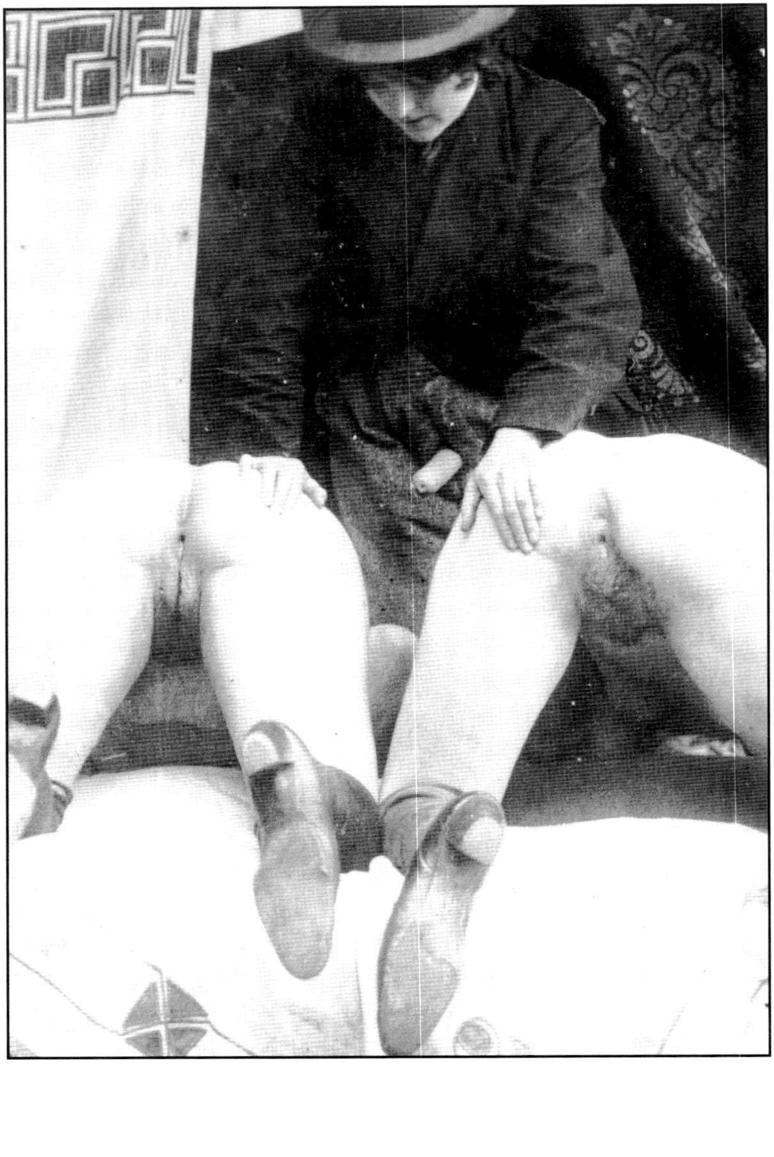